The Beginning of Leaving

ALSO BY ELSA VALMIDIANO
We Are No Longer Babaylan

THE BEGINNING OF LEAVING

Elsa Valmidiano

QUERENCIA

Querencia Press, LLC
Chicago, Illinois

for my folks, Elsie and Albérto
&
for those who leave, and must

No sáan nga makaammó nga nangtaliáw ti naggapuánna, saán
a makadánon ti papanánna.

They who do not look back to their origins will not reach their
destination.

—Sarsarita, Ilocano proverb

CONTENTS

AUTHOR'S NOTE

These essays reveal *my* truth where I do not speak on behalf of anyone else's. The stories recounted in these essays include the lived experiences of those who lived them, as witnessed by me or revealed to me. They also include details as I best remember them. The names and characteristics of some individuals in this book have been changed. All photographs included in this collection belong to me except otherwise noted by "photo courtesy of."

FOREWORD

The "journey" is an ancient and popular metaphor in the human narrative. A journey in search of a better life, as escape, or as hunger represents a deep imperative in humans to physically survive and thrive. It can also be a way to fulfill emotional, psychological, and intellectual needs. Often, there is a focus on destination, the end of a journey and the potential fulfillment of a dream.

The title of Elsa Valmidiano's collection of essays, *The Beginning of Leaving*, points the reader to the moment of decision-making and action. An open-ended term, "leaving" implies hope, seeking — and consequences. Departure is also letting go of something, however difficult that may be. What does it mean to carefully place your foot upon the ground, or to "hit the ground running" — knowing that what you encounter will change you, perhaps significantly? Later, in looking back on the journey — one reviews what happened, choosing what truths to reveal or suppress. And once we know the truth, how will we hold it?

These essays set off on routes familiar to most Filipinos and already taken by many — though not all — of Valmidiano's family members, a people whose archipelagic history has run the gamut of peaceful exchange through language and culture as well as revolt against colonial violence and domination. The journeys are not only "diasporic" — but also journeys of escape and confrontation, exploration, healing, and renewal. The author follows her own paths to understand how those histories of departure are entwined with her own.

One lesson that leaving teaches is the value of home and security. But what if you long for or embrace more than one home? Valmidiano is a global traveler. Her infancy was spent in the Philippines in Las Piñas, "in the subdivision of Moonwalk on Soyuz Street." A place where streets are named after spaceships and imbued with the desire to escape gravity. She thinks of home as Carson, California, yet, she professes "a love, longing, and fascination for our Motherland," the Philippines. For her mother, Ubbog, La Union, is home, a place her daughter can touch through mother, family members, and ancestors.

Writing is often like detective work, and Valmidiano is indefatigable. While visiting her parents' ancestral homes and talking to relatives, her explorations of family, its threads of belonging and trauma, are persistent. Laying in bed with her Lola Fely, she writes, "Stories were buried in her body. I wanted them." The author moves ever forward; with words she gently prods at painful memories (including her own), pulls back, collects traces of those who suffered, those who disappeared, and those who survived. In the process, the author also explores her own very personal routes through wonder and grief, birth and death.

Memories of closeness seem key here. The physical and sensory experience of family, embodied in greetings, the *mano po*, the touches and sniff-kissing:

> As the elders come out of their homes to greet us, there is a combination of performing the mano po and swooping me, my older brother, and two sisters into their arms, inhaling us very hard. There's kissing, hugging, and inhaling, a combination of all three, burying their noses several times into our cheeks and breathing in our scent. It seems we disappear into their lungs.

Physical connection, "skinship," is significant throughout these essays, as are the moments of wrenching, personal and physical loss. Valmidiano dwells in such moments, or sites—the "diasporic body"—while showing us how the actions and outcomes of colonial and capitalist systems and white supremacy have exerted forces on minds and bodies through generations. How it shocks and scars, shames or silences us and our forebears—although, with luck and courage, time may release the stories that we take with us into the world.

Spirituality and long-held beliefs, too, exert an influence, whether as a rebellion against institutions, balm for loneliness, or as reminders to respect ancestors and their sacred lands. Family members long gone appear again as ghosts to portend important events, or to greet and carry away those who, in dying, depart this world.

These essays are particularly relevant for women navigating the current anti-abortion movement in the United States and other countries. Valmidiano relates her experience as a child with anti-abortion "sex education" in a Catholic school—the beginning of trauma that would extend to her early experiences with sex and abortion, and even into her workplace. Because of her experience as a reproductive-rights activist and counselor in the Philippines, her writing is especially tuned in to women's experiences of birth and death, whether writing about her own abortion and post-abortion experience, and its spiritual dimensions, or the birth of her mother during World War II in the Philippines.

Diasporic tales can be revelatory, but such stories—for victims and conquerors as well as those who dwell in the liminal seas between one culture and another—do not always lead to resolution. The reality of trauma, lingering through generations, does not always allow it. Sometimes one *must* leave. Sometimes, grief is the only healing. This is why writers like Valmidiano—who dare to voice the *dung-aw*—who look back and follow the tracks of departure, both painful and promising, are necessary.

I grew up in postwar housing in the US, almost completely isolated and independent from extended family. My mother and I were the family unit. Period. But there was another "family" across the ocean, *sa Pilipinas*, which seemed to be primarily my mother's—accessed only through letters and the rare phone call. My father, too, as a crew member on a merchant marine ship, was always overseas. So, I'm struck by Valmidiano's ability to reach out empathically and connect with individuals in her family, even those she has never met, but can imagine, and to see herself in their shared history and *kapwa*—shared identity—and touch their lives. How does one begin? Perhaps by reciting the names of places and people: Ubbog and Lapog, Quezon City, Aotearoa, Tbilisi, Lisbon, Tacloban, Oakland; Lilong Tito, Lola Fely, Lola Ising, Lilang Poten, Martinez Valmidiano . . .

There are many powerful moments in this book, embodied in the author's writing-to-understand how the colonial encounter is passed on through generations in our bodily experience; how trauma is dealt with—through suppression or empathy, projection onto others, or via exploration and the curiosity-driven work of writing. Just as powerful are the processes of healing, which I think these essays represent.

The Beginning of Leaving should be considered an invitation for you to explore your own departures and arrivals, family and ancestral histories—not just the stories that you have been told, but the silences, which are also speaking.

— Jean Vengua is a Filipinx American visual artist and writer. She is the author of Marcelina *(Paloma Press),* Prau *(Meritage Press),* The Aching Vicinities *(Otoliths Press), and* Corporeal *(Black Radish Books). Dr. Vengua's poetry and essays are widely published in journals and anthologies. She has taught at UC Berkeley, UC Santa Cruz, CSU Monterey Bay, and Gavilan College.*

WHAT WE WERE MEANT TO

Are we born feet first
to hit the ground running
our hearts already exposed
slashed open to bleed?

See this hair:
> a growth of tendrils.

See this face:
> my foot emerging.

See these eyes:
> my toes.

See this rigid chin:
> the heel of my foot.

See this cheek:
> the palm of my foot

not feeling the caress of your hand
but Earth herself, to walk her body, and
this is the way she cradles me
in the valley of her mountains' embrace
sings me lullabies with the roar of her oceans
and runs her fingers through my leafy hair
as her kisses are the wind rustling through trees.

I am born this diasporic foot.

But do you see two perfectly formed heads
or are they bulbs emerging from the birth canal
like Jacob and Esau, where a white god dictated
one must be the underdog
when maybe our ancestors narrate us
as simply community
our collective foot delivering us
to new destinations together?

Ilocana Nanangs of Old say that
children born feet first have the ability to
save you from choking on a fish bone by
lightly stroking your throat
when maybe those who choke have
stayed or tarried too long
when the fish bone — well —
don't fish live in the sea
where we are meant to be
and the fish bone tickles you
                nudges you

to leave *for god's sakes already*
        by boat
        by legs
        and this diasporic foot
                my foot
              your foot
              our face?

Can you tell we are smiling, crying
pulled by the foot from the birth canal
to just go?

Blood drop, teardrop
down our slashed heart cheek
or maybe it's our bleeding mouth
barely open to protest what
we were born to do.

See our 7,000 leafy tendrils
interwoven with water as
a swirling grid of streets
we were meant to
                    cross.

Nectar *by Andrea Guerrero, 11 in x 14 in, graphite on paper, 2021*

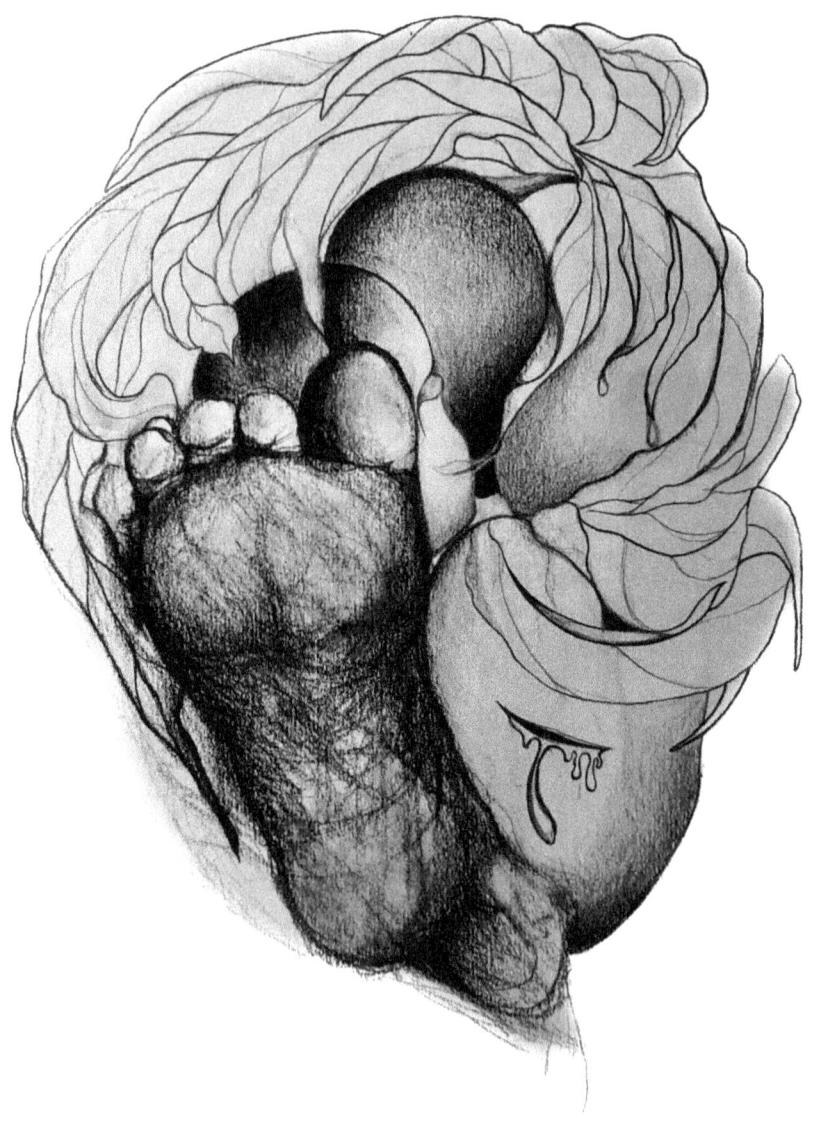

FIRST HOME

My father tells me I was almost born in our red jeep. The red jeep stalled on the expressway while my mother was in labor. She had been getting ready for work that morning when contractions began at 7 AM. Both she and my father worked at the Bureau of Soils in Metro Manila. It would've been my mother's last day at the Planning Department before going on maternity leave.

But I wasn't born in the red jeep. I was born at the closest hospital off the expressway in Parañaque, near where the red jeep stalled. I should've been born at the hospital where my older siblings were born, but my urgency of being delivered into the world would not allow that. The hospital at the nearest expressway exit would have to do. I was born ten minutes after my mother made her way past the hospital doors. By the time I was four, I was madly in love with the color red.

We lived in a two-bedroom home with a large kitchen in the subdivision of Moonwalk on Soyuz Street in the then-municipality of Las Piñas. Las Piñas was not a city yet. Our street was named after a 1960s Soviet rocket. All the street names in our neighborhood had astronautical associations to spacecrafts and rockets from the 60s reflecting the Space Race between the US and the Soviet Union—Apollo, Orbiter, Skynet, Explorer, Mariner, Pioneer, Titan, Luna, Mercury Atlas, Iris, Ranger, Nimbus, and Early Bird. The street names would not sound Filipino at all. America would already colonize my infancy and would embed itself as a purpose, its own Space Race, where you could always race to be better than someone else, or be better than who you thought yourself to be, to the moon and back, or at least trying to gain passage to the United States of America.

My infant self would already sojourn to Cubao and Project 8 in Quezon City to visit my Lola Fely, aunts, uncles, and countless cousins. I suffered my first car accident with my family at an intersection a block from my Lola Fely's house — her beautiful house she had built in 1950 after the War, after losing her husband to the War — sold in 2011, torn down in 2012. A multi-story hotel now rests in its place with broken doors and cockroach infestations. My Lola Fely's beautiful house, not even an echo in what is presently there.

Between my birth to sixteen-months-old, my parents never brought me to the home of our ancestors — La Union and Ilocos Sur — as they planned and prepared for their final departure from the Motherland.

While they could not bring me to our ancestral barangays, Ubbog and Labnig, Ubbog and Labnig were still brought to me — through the sweet coos between my infant self and Lola Ising visiting from Ubbog, and through the sniff-kisses from Lilang Atang visiting from Labnig. Through my grandmothers' hugs and kisses, the land of my ancestors could still embrace me with a final goodbye before we left for good.

Rice paddies, vegetable farms, jeepneys, pedicabs, Mass every Sunday, big family get-togethers, a father working overseas in Sumatra-Kuala Lumpur-Saskatoon-Edmonton-Red Deer-Calgary-Los Angeles, a mother working late nights in Manila with a long commute home, a few yayas, and doting grandparents, were what made Las Piñas home.

Las Piñas was my home for my first sixteen months, the home of infant dreams, where memories dissolved before they could materialize into words. Displacement eventually found its way in a restless sixteen-month-old, traveling to new places in crowded airports and crowded airplanes. From

Honolulu to LAX, my mother would cradle me in her arms, trying to soothe my bloodcurdling screams for five-and-a-half hours without pause. "You were very tired but just couldn't sleep," my mother told me.

Could I have been missing Ináng-bayan but unable to say so in words?

Had my infant self thought it a dirty trick, when more than twenty-four hours had passed and we were still on a plane, not yet understanding that we were never returning Home?

In less than ten years after my birth, Las Piñas, amidst the Marcos Regime, would become something other than Home, as surrounding rice paddies and farms would be swallowed by concrete, making way for the rapid development of dense, new cities that would proliferate at reckless speed.

I cannot tell you what Las Piñas air smelled like before we left—possibly a mixture of campfire, of a pig or goat roasting over an open spit, pink plumerias, sweet mangoes, banana leaves, ripe sun-kissed vegetables from the garden, freshly chopped sitaw under a faucet of cold running water, clean laundry hanging on a clothesline, and a pot of just cooked rice.

I cannot tell you what Las Piñas noises sounded like before we left—possibly the languid rustle of banana leaves in the afternoon breeze, the endless *cockle doodle doo*'s from the neighborhood roosters, and the excited staccato Tagalog chatter from small children playing in the street.

Infant memory only presents itself as a hallucination when I have visited the Motherland as an adult, or when I experience fleeting moments wherever I have lain my head to rest—in Carson, San Diego, Auckland, Dampier, DC, Syracuse, Quezon City, Tacloban, Lisbon, Tbilisi, and

Oakland—when certain smells and sounds become a nostalgic ache for the things I swear I have touched only in my dreams, crushing my infantile amnesia, and rushing through me like déjà vu.

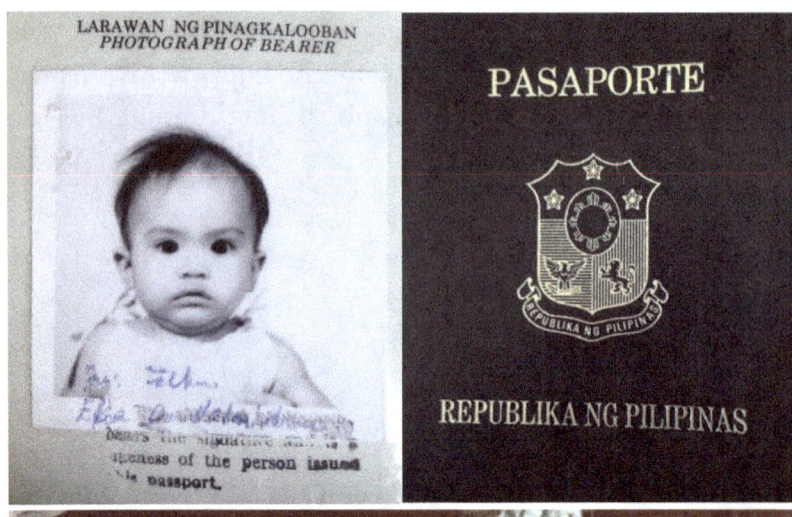

Top: Philippine passport photo, 1978
Bottom: Lola Ben, my mother, me, and Lola Ising, Manila Airport, the day
we immigrated, 1979

ASWANG HUNGER

From Manila to Labnig, I watch the road as it twists and turns. I stare at the banana trees running alongside the road and notice their gentle rustle and sway as our jeepney speeds by. I cannot see the beginning nor end of where we are heading.

When the road opens up, we pass a man being hauled in a cart by a carabao alongside the rice paddies, which stretch for miles like the ocean. The carabao's horns circle their head like huge boomerangs. They move slowly, like they are taking a relaxed stroll. My mother says, "They are gentle and can take a beating so many times before they break, but watch out for the carabao that loses it!"

The humming of the jeepney engine becomes part of everything around us. The quiet whisper of the paddies becomes evident when Uncle Siano finally parks and shuts off the engine. We take a bathroom break and grab merienda off the side of the road.

Uncle Siano loves The Eagles. We've been listening to "Hotel California" on his cassette tape over and over again since leaving Manila. Either that, or he doesn't have any other cassettes to play.

"What do you think the song means? What do you think 'the beast' is? Satan, duh!" my seventeen-year-old brother educates my ten-year-old self. Hopefully we won't be seeing any Hotel Californias along a dark paddy highway.

We are heading to Labnig, my father's barrio, which belongs to the town of Lapog, but they changed the name to San Juan in 1961.

My father explains, "If you said you were from Lapog, it was notorious as a rough town where people killed each other. It was full of gangs and crimes. The people in charge thought changing the name would sanitize it. Lapog was also known for its smallpox epidemic, and no one wanted to be remembered for that."

My grandfather, Lilong Tito, had contracted smallpox as a little boy. His youngest brother, Alvero, had died from it at seven-years-old. I vaguely remember the small circles on the sides of Lilong's face. They were barely visible and I mistook them as birthmarks, but my father said they were from smallpox. Lilong suffered only a mild case, whereas others suffered horrifically. If it didn't kill you, the deadly disease forever scarred the beautiful faces and bodies of countless young people. Our grandmother's cousin had contracted such a bad case that she lost her eyesight as a result.

It seems the name change worked, as my father attests that most people have forgotten the horrific associations to what happened in Lapog. However, the elders never forget.

As we finally arrive in Labnig after eight hours on the road, lush rolling hills surround us. It is the middle of August, 1988, two years after the EDSA Revolution. At ten-years-old, I cannot tell if there is any change in the people since the fall of their leader who comes from these very parts. If anything, there is a timelessness here. Development seems scarce, giving me the impression that much hasn't changed since my father left the barrio two decades ago.

My paternal grandfather is a Martinez Valmidiano. My paternal grandmother is a Somera Torres. The families have been in Labnig for centuries.

Three houses off the main dirt road run alongside the rice paddies where we are staying with Lilang Poten for the next few days. Poten is our grandmother's youngest sister who never married. Lilang Poten's two-story house stands separate from the other homes, but they all share the same yard with no fences marking whose property belongs to whom. Chickens, goats, carabao, dogs, and land seem equally shared among all. Upstairs, an old painting of her mother, our great-grandmother, Lilang Sabina, watches over you while you sleep.

Upon our arrival, all the children from the barrio come out to see us. They don't approach us but follow our every move as we are shown around.

My father unpacks the Balikbayan boxes and passes around soap, shampoo, washcloths, and the rest of its contents to everyone. I had never seen kids so excited to receive a bar of soap. It's like Christmas. Each kid cups their own bar as if they were holding a precious bunny rabbit, caressing it against their cheeks, and taking long sniffs of their Irish Spring, Dial, and Ivory soap bars.

At first their squeals and ecstatic laughter over soap seem silly to my ten-year-old self, until I notice their flimsy flip-flops, their worn-out and faded shirts, and their shorts with gaping holes.

It surprises me that most of the children wear our clothes from when we were very little—my Cabbage Patch Kids tennis shoes from when I was five, now on the feet of a little boy; my brother's white and blue Snoopy T-shirt, now on another little boy. After all the times when a neighbor or family friend or relative went to the Philippines with a Balikbayan box packed with all our old clothes, we discover this is where it all went—here, to this barrio, to these children wearing our clothes that are clearly out-of-date and out-offashion back home in LA. They run around playing in our old clothes, sending flashes of who we used to be.

As the elders come out of their homes to greet us, there is a combination of performing the mano po and swooping me, my older brother, and two sisters into their arms, inhaling us very hard. There's kissing, hugging, and inhaling, a combination of all three, burying their noses several times into our cheeks and breathing in our scent. It seems we disappear into their lungs.

The second floor of Lilang Poten's house is an enormous loft-style room. With the exception of my parents who sleep on a tattered bed in the right corner by the window, my siblings, relatives, and myself sleep on a banig on the Narra wood floor.

The rest of the house has windows but no glass in them. They are simply outlets for air, offering relief, especially at night to the sleepers who otherwise would suffocate under the heat and humidity. There's no bathroom but a small closet-like space in the corner of the second floor, concealed by a red curtain which hides an empty metal pail and a separate basin of water.

To bathe, there are two options. The first option is just outside Lilang Poten's house: a stall made up of bamboo walls no taller than six feet on all three sides. A small spigot is located near one's knees with an empty bucket. Where a door would've been, the bather stands exposed. To conceal one's nakedness, you must crouch perfectly, knees tucked to your chest, and the soles of your feet planted flat on the floor. From the spigot, you must quickly fill a bucket and tabo-tabo—pour buckets of cold water over your head.

My father, me, my brother, and Lola Fely, Labnig rice paddies, 1988

The second option is going to a relative's house down the road with a bathroom that is part of their house. It is the best bathroom in the entire barrio as they have a toilet that is *not* a cemented hole in the middle of a field, curtained off by a flimsy cloth held up by bamboo sticks. There is the privacy of an actual room with a water pump for bathing, fully equipped with a faucet, toilet bowl, bathtub, and toilet paper. It is clean. It reminds me of a huge janitor's closet with plain cement walls. One must dump buckets of water into the toilet bowl in order for it to flush. You must never throw toilet paper into the bowl. My father laughs. Growing up, there was no such thing as toilet paper. Only banana leaves.

During our stay, my father brings us to the site of his childhood home situated on the other side of the rice paddies. The dirt road running alongside the houses is muddy but fine like butter due to the previous night's rain. We each carry boxes full of Marlboro cigarettes. The red and white boxes are bigger than shoeboxes. They are for our uncles, our father's cousins, who live on the other side of the barrio. My father is full of stories, sharing in an excited voice how these were the same rice paddies he had waded in decades and decades ago as a boy.

As we pass a carabao, my father tells us the story of when he was about five and had been riding on the back of his carabao, the huge beast unexpectedly stumbled and came crashing down on him at which he thought the beast had killed him. His laugh booms.

We get to a small turn-off from the main road, make a right, and hike up a small dirt path opening up to, what looks like, a little village with brown shacks. They are scattered. My father's sister warns, "Maybe we will go hunting for smurfs. Be careful. They live here, in the trees," she points with her puckered lips.

"Are they blue and do they sing la-la-la-la-la-la?" my brother asks.

My sisters and I laugh when our aunt responds, "Blue, green, red, they live here, in the hills, in the trees, you will see," pointing with her puckered lips at all the trees hovering above us. "There's aswang and ansisit."

When we arrive at the site, the only things left to my surprise are the first three cement steps of a staircase and the foundation covered with cracks like endless veins and arteries. I question my father about the absence of the house. Lilong had sold the home, and then it was torn down before he and my grandmother immigrated to California. The house was built in 1953, though my father also guesses it was 1949. Their old house and new house were built adjacent to each other, and the first three cement steps were from the new house.

Lilong had built his family home with the help of his Bayanihan and my father, nine at the time, a little man, cutting down bamboo in the community forest when everyone could still gather all that they needed. This house would be a triumph, a place to finally call home after years of escaping the Japanese during the War, hiding in the mountains, my father born during that evacuation, his birthplace unknown, possibly a chicken coop, where home was a safety zone in the mountains, a hiding place for years, and home was in the body of a father and mother and two sisters to an infant boy born on the run. The end of the War meant finally being safe to come down the mountain and build a home in the land of their ancestors.

There was never any electricity or running water. Light was only available through kerosene lamp and water gathered at a well, up until the house was sold and razed to the ground in the 1980s. My father emphasizes, *The house had a cement foundation*, which may not mean much to those who take the construction of houses for granted these days.

I watch my father and his sister pace around the ruins as if they were examining a dining room in a kitchen. They reenact scenes of their childhood, standing where their dining table used to be and miming how they would race to finish all of the food off the table lest someone be the last who doesn't have enough to eat. My father and aunt still see the house as if it were an apparition, while we see nothing but an empty cement stage surrounded by an overgrowth of tall coconut and mango trees. As an adult twenty years later, I will eventually return and pay homage to the remaining cement steps of this long forgotten home.

My father passes around the boxes of Marlboro cigarettes to the uncles who are gathered around the ruins. I can't help but ask my father, "Why do you buy them so many?"

"Cigarettes are expensive here. American cigarettes are what they like, balasang co."

That afternoon, my father talks a lot and laughs a lot on that cracked cement stage, reminiscing about his childhood in the barrio.

"When I was your age," he begins in English, carefully enunciating each consonant and vowel in his strong Ilocano accent, "I was already living away from home. High school was in the neighboring town. Oh, how I cried and cried for my parents. The town kids laughed at me for wearing the same clothes every day. I beat them to the ground with my stick. You know, the branch I had snapped off a tree!" my father laughs. It's hard to imagine my father ever crying or being bullied. He continues, "I had one pair of pants. When I got home from school, your Lilang made me remove them. I had to walk around the house with my butó hanging out. She didn't want me to get my only pair dirty!"

As I overhear my father reminisce with his cousins, I can't speak the language, but I understand what they're saying.

In Labnig, there is a softness and ease with my father. Here, he is not a looming authority figure demanding excellence. Here, he is welcomed and admired by his kin. Here, he is simply a man reaching for the past of what brought him joy. Here, he is everything he is not in America. Here, he is not a scientist with accolades. Here, he is still a simple barrio boy where dreams are great and lofty, and almost impossible.

Between farming and school in Lapog and Cabugao, Little Albérto would've climbed to a vista point overlooking the Labnig horizon. He would've looked beyond the fields and fields of rice paddies, and wondered, and knew, that there must be so much more than this. That there was a bigger life to be had beyond the barrio.

There is a small respite for his children to get to see this other side of their father, albeit temporarily.

Merienda approaches when one of my small cousins, about twelve-years-old, climbs the tall coconut tree and fetches coconuts. He gracefully scampers up the tree. The rough palms of his feet lightly scrape against the tree trunk. He plucks a coconut with a small knife. I am sure my father climbed this same coconut tree when he was a handsome little boy with no shoes, no shirt, who went to school with town bullies. Those same bullies who owned head-to-toe outfits, unlike my father who owned only one.

"Between farming and school in Lapog and Cabugao, Little Albérto would've climbed to a vista point overlooking the Labnig horizon. He would've looked beyond the fields and fields of rice paddies, and wondered, and knew, that there must be so much more than this. That there was a bigger life to be had beyond the barrio."

Labnig landscape, 2009

Three coconuts are thrown down which my father catches. My father, the Ivy League graduate and former United Nations Environmental officer, punctures the tough green husks with his pocketknife, the tart juice leaking out into glasses. He splits each empty coconut open to have the sweet, white flesh scooped out and eaten. "This is nutritious," he says. The coconut juice tastes like sugar water while the flesh is sweet and milky.

My eight-year-old sister and I play with the other children. One of them is a four-year-old girl who has an adorable raspy voice and follows me and my sister around like she is our little personal assistant. Though she doesn't live at Lilang Poten's house, she sleeps there every night to be close to me and my sister, sharing our banig on the bare wooden floorboards. She doesn't hide her excitement as she shares sleeping space with her older cousins from America, her raspy voice telling stories while she lays next to us before we all fall asleep. She and the other children only speak Ilocano while my sister and I only speak English. We barely understand each other in our attempts to try and communicate in broken English or broken Ilocano, but our play together doesn't require many words and makes us equally close in just a few days. A sixteen-year-old cousin named Teresing shows us around the barrio and speaks English very well. She tries her best to teach us Ilocano and speaks Ilocanglish, hoping we will catch on.

Most of my cousins' curiosity revolves around our lives in America. In their eyes, we are high class Amerikanos living in LA with the movie stars and fancy cars. But LA is not Hollywood or fancy cars. LA is the quiet city of Carson. LA is where the ARCO refinery is within view of our bungalow home. LA is where the smog is. LA is where our run-down lime-green shag carpet lies on the living room floor. I want to tell them, "That's LA."

During a trip by myself to Labnig while on a months-long sabbatical in the Philippines twenty years later, I will see my cousins for the second time in my life and learn from them how my father had helped to financially supplement many of their educations, hoping to give them the same opportunities he had so they could excel outside of the barrio. Some will have gone on to higher education and careers, while others will remain in the barrio, having dropped out of school, married, raising several children, and carrying on the farming tradition of our ancestors. As word gets out that my adult self has returned to Labnig, many will come up to me, now in their thirties, and will say effusively over and over again, "Tell your dad thanks," when I never would have known of his generosity.

For our last dinner—a despedida—residents from the three homes gather at Lilang Poten's house with one light bulb and three lanterns to share. During the few days in my father's barrio, I never figure out who the true residents of Lilang Poten's house are. Since we're in town, everyone is gathered here every night. After tonight, it's a slow and bumpy eight-hour drive in a jeepney from Labnig to Quezon City for another week and on a flight back to LA.

One step of a staircase of my father's childhood home remains, Labnig, Ilocos Sur, 2009. A photograph of the bamboo house exists but I do not have permission to share it.

Photographed here during a trip by myself to Labnig while on a months-long sabbatical in the Philippines in 2009: 20.5 years later after my first trip to Labnig with my family. With my Valmidiano and Torres aunts and cousins and their children, Labnig, Ilocos Sur, 2009

This evening, it rains. Lizards race across the ceiling. The table is laden with grilled Blue Marlin, Chicken Tinola, Papaitan, and several gulay dishes: Monggo, Pinakbet, Paksiw, Dinengdeng, and Guisadong Upo. Fish is caught at Solot Solot, the neighboring beach a couple of miles from here. There's no refrigeration in the barrio. Meals are fresh with everything caught and gathered that day.

Since we've been here, we've had to eat with our hands, with the exception of stews like Tinola or Sinigang when we're offered spoons, but outside of that, the only spoons available are the big serving spoons to scoop your own personal portion. My parents never warned us about eating with our hands in the barrio. When we sat down to our first meal, they began plowing through with fluid hands like old pros.

My parents, aunts, and uncles all laughed at our initial clumsiness as my siblings and I tried to pick up rice in our hands. The other dishes weren't as difficult as we were long accustomed to picking our chicken and fish off the bone with our hands anyway, no matter how "Americanized" our relatives assumed us to be. However, the rice felt impossible.

After carefully watching my parents eat their rice, never touching the palm of their hand but neatly packed into a little mass between their thumb and the tips of their fingers, my siblings and I eventually got it. We ate with ease as if we'd done it all our lives. There were no applause or praise once we figured it out. Rather, the adults ignored us, speaking in Ilocano among themselves while waving their hands in symphony with a little mass of balled-up rice held in the tips of their fingers and thumb. Now, on our last night, we eat like true inapoy champions.

After dinner, my family spends our last night with our countless relatives whom we wonder when we'll ever see again. Between the storytelling and the jokes, I can't help but focus on the dark corners of Lilang Poten's sala and wonder if I am seeing things or if I am truly seeing the images of my ancestors with their tan faces, chiseled arms, calloused fingers, calloused toes, and their teeth amber-stained with betel nut.

In one corner, a barefoot, toothless aunt stands severely hunched over. She is one of my father's eldest cousins. Dirt is buried deep beneath her fingernails. Her eyes are faded to a pale blue. Her fingers and toes are gnarled by the toil of farm life, while I must look like Ms. Filipina-Americana with soft hands and soft feet.

Everyone here is embraced by the barrio heat and immune from the ruthless mosquitoes who refuse their blood. These same relatives, unafraid of the dark, have skin that carries the fragrance of rice paddies, sweat, and humidity. These farmers know nothing of universities, Jimi Hendrix, Shakespeare, computers, condoms, but only this life that gives them the stroking sun, swaying banana leaves, coconuts, tobacco fields, rice paddies, typhoons, sex, the China Sea, carabao, riyari, goats, dogs, fiestas, aswang, kapre, ansisit, and marmarna.

The only thing true here is the ansisit who are afraid of the city and choose to remain with these simple wise men and where strong women breastfeed their babies without shame.

No one speaks English in this space, just Ilocano.

No one speaks about vanishing albolaryo as the albolaryo are still *here*. They go about their plant magic with cayanga blossoms, bayabas leaves, and makabuhay. They go about their prayers to a Christian god—*Ay Apo*—but also ward off ansisit and marmarna who live in the baliti trees and the soil—*cayo cayo umadayo cayo*. They go about worshipping statues of saints and Mary and Christ who mystify little kids when adults know this is how age-old adoration of original deities is hidden in plain sight. They go about their anting-anting steeped into their pockets or worn as jewelry which carries a power that houses the spirits of all we love and lose and still hold dear.

Ghosts of our ancestors linger within these walls, like when I was five and the world fell away. We had been living in LA then.

I was in the hallway of our house when the voices came. This was not the first time. They were sirens trapped inside my head. Panic set in but I didn't scream. I sat down, leaned my back against the wall, tucked my knees to my chest, wrapped my arms around my legs, bowed my head, and closed my eyes. "Stop talking to me, please," I whispered. The voices were a mix of static, of too many trying to speak at once, spinning, spinning. I never understood what they were trying to tell me. The next thing I knew, I opened my eyes to find my mother knelt down before me. "Are you alright? Does your head hurt?" I could not explain what had just happened except her presence and voice pulled me back from that dark tesseract of a thousand voices.

The voices then stopped and never returned.

I thought if I listened hard enough, I'd hear them again, but I never did. I didn't realize how much I would miss the simultaneous whirring of their voices, all trying to tell me something at the same dizzying time. I would spend the rest of my adulthood disentangling what I could remember of their voices, giving each a chance to have their stories heard.

When Spain arrived, it was unnecessary to recap the past to children. They had endured the same struggles as their parents. Together, they had survived colonization, smallpox, war, rape, and forced migrations. The elders would grow old while their children grew up silent and ashamed of their own Brown skin and suffering under Spanish, British, American, and Japanese imperialists. Those same children would then raise their children without telling them stories of their past. Their children desiring better prospects beyond the barrio, or simply because they were forced off their land, would migrate to other provinces like Pangasinan and Nueva Ecija or to big cities like Manila, Cebu, and Davao. Then their children would migrate to even bigger cities across the sea like Honolulu, Seattle, San Francisco, Los Angeles, Dallas, New York, Chicago, London, Perth, Adelaide, Dubai, Milan. Great-great-grandchildren would be born elsewhere never setting foot on the islands and never learning the struggles of their ancestors. The old people full of stories and revolutionary spirit would eventually die off in the barrio, while immigrant elders abroad were no longer affectionately greeted with the mano po by their foreign-born grandchildren. Teenage descendants in America, like me and my siblings, would be left scrounging for pieces of our heritage, while those indifferent would grow up obsessing over the kind of cars they drove, the latest in Calvin Klein, the latest technology, and hating the look of their skin, eyes, and nose.

Is it possible that the age at which my parents started dreaming of America is the same age where I feel a tie to this land; to return? They feel they no longer belong here. That we no longer belong here.

There are still spaces here. And yet I know something out here is craving big cars, big streets, and big city lights.

The land is rice paddies, but there is hunger in the air. The same hunger felt at my maternal grandmother's house, when my mother told us it was once rice paddies everywhere in Cubao. The industrial hunger doesn't come from the rice paddies but from the creeping of those sneaky in their demand for change.

My father warns against my questions about why we never stayed. "They can cut you down and shut you up. Whenever someone does good in the world, it's dangerous. You can only have so much until everything collapses around you."

My father knows something I don't.

We left and are leaving again.

It's so beautiful here. I will miss this. This. This. Everything. But this is not what my father wanted for us. I still ask, *Why couldn't we have everything, here? Did we sell out by moving to America, the country that colonized us for almost five decades and denied us our freedom and independence?*

I still ask.

As laughter and stories boom from every corner of the house, it feels as if everyone is looking at me and my siblings, their eyes sunken in from hard work and hunger, an aswang hunger that starves for our sweet American blood, one last time.

ONE HUNDRED AND EIGHTY EGGS

Thirteen. Fourteen. Fifteen. Sixteen. Seventeen. Eighteen. Nineteen.

Each age a reminder when twelve eggs per year escaped from house arrest. Eighty-four eggs. Released.

Sent off with a warm red farewell.

Twenty. Twenty-one. Twenty-two. Twenty-three. Twenty-four. Twenty-five. Twenty-six. Twenty-seven. Twenty-eight. Twenty-nine. Thirty. Thirty-one. Thirty-two. Thirty-three. Thirty-four.

Each age a reminder when the pill was a prison guard to twelve eggs per year whose sentence has been commuted inside me. One hundred and eighty eggs. Waiting for release.

Oocyte. Ootid. Ovum.

O.

I wOke up to the realization of the One hundred and eighty eggs waiting their turn after fifteen years, and I am wondering if it is fair to have cheated Mother Nature.

I consider the weight of countless childbirths and clandestine abortions — ten, eleven, twelve, thirteen, fourteen — that broke the bodies of so many maternal ancestors.

As a 21st century descendant, there is phenomenal no-strings-attached sex. Not getting pregnant. Choosing my own life over the existence of a new one that could drastically change the direction of mine.

That could drastically change me.

Orgasm. Opportunity. Option.

O.

I chOse me but   did I leave my bOdy behind?

I used to think the pill was magical until I realized what it was doing to make my body stop.

I used to think the pill was magical until I realized whose bodies — poor / Black / Brown / institutionalized / incarcerated — were tested upon to make their bodies stop.

No one talks about the brain fog, the chemical numbness, or the sensation of watching your life play before you as if on a television screen on an indescribably slanted floor. This is not the solution either.

We've been allowed to go forward with our lives, direct our own paths, be ambitious in our careers, travel the world alone, take up lovers and leave 'em, and I'm still all for it, except a chemical wall I find hard to trust has my mind scrambling, while my body is telling me She is tired of waiting.

And when you decide to stop cheating Mother Nature, the eggs are ready to go.

I don't mean getting pregnant but ready to do what they have been waiting to do — finally release.

But the blood has been dissipating.

At fifteen, a warm gush would happen between my legs, when pads would get soaked, and I would have to change them every four hours. Twenty years later, the chemical wall has laid out bricks of unsullied pads as if waiting for rain.

No gush. No warmth. No rain.

If only we could have our cake and eat it too.

Complaints continue with the hassle of the period. The heaviness. The cramps. The bloating. The mood swings. The headaches. The leakage scares. The body's natural way of cleansing itself every month and starting anew.

The aborting of an old self at the end of each month.

Or maybe the birthing of a new self at each beginning.

Now as each month rolls into the next, days become one month, two, three, and then fifteen years — for ambition, career, sex, travel — while the body is left weeping like a five-year-old abandoned on the swings.

The birth would've been that day, I was sure of it.

After my first semester in New Zealand was over, I had decided to visit relatives over the winter break in Australia, when one July night, flying from Sydney to Perth, I looked at the stars through my window seat, the moon, the darkness, the Southern Cross, and cried inside as if the whole world were spinning and the plane was about to crash. But it was just me crashing as I suddenly remembered it would have been the baby's due date. I would relive the memory when my boyfriend had taken me to my appointment as I sat uncomfortably next to a woman in her eighth month for her prenatal appointment, while I had been there to end my pregnancy.

At twenty, I had an abortion, and for ten months afterward, suffered trauma. How do I explain it? I didn't want to be sad. I didn't want to cry every night for hours. I didn't want to get up at 4 PM. But those things happened. My emotions took over and trying to keep busy felt like I was dragging my feet.

Is there a link between abortion and trauma? For me, the answer is yes. It still remains difficult to say I suffered trauma after my abortion as I fear I am somehow criticizing a fundamental right I so fiercely believe in. I question what a pro-choice person is supposed to look like.

Am I a bad pro-choicer?

Under the pro-life movement, the subject of trauma has become a weapon against the pro-choice movement. Post-Abortion Syndrome, specifically coined by the pro-life movement, has been used to perpetuate the myth that abortion is a harmful procedure resulting in regret and depression. If we applied the same mental health reasoning of post-partum depression to pregnancy, no woman would ever want to become pregnant. As investigated by the American Psychological Association, Post-Abortion Syndrome is scientifically proven to not exist as the immediate result of all abortions, just as much as post-partum depression does not exist as the immediate result of all births.

When I had my abortion, I had just turned twenty, still one of my more memorable birthdays. Though I couldn't admit it to myself then, I had an abusive boyfriend who forced me to have sex. Rape would be the appropriate term to describe this, but even still, that is a hard word for me to say.

He was Indian and Hindu. His parents disapproved of my being Filipina and Catholic. My own parents didn't know he existed. It's not that I wasn't allowed to date. Boys and dating were nonexistent topics growing up. You studied hard, got straight A's, and went to college. Anything outside of that was extraneous. But my traumatic experience with an unwanted pregnancy and abortion began way before my abusive relationship in college. It began in childhood.

Childhood consisted of pro-life propaganda starting at age nine. Catholic school was twelve long years in the LA suburbs. The student body of my Catholic elementary school was predominantly Filipino and Mexican, the children of first-generation immigrants. By age twelve, the infamous year of finally learning where babies come from, my parents, our parents, handed over the reins of their child's sex education to my Catholic school, thereby ceding absolute control to include abortion as part of the curriculum. We learned more about abortion than sex itself. Sex Ed should've been renamed Abortion Ed. None of the parents were explicitly informed that graphic pictures and videos of mutilated fetuses would be part of Sex Ed.

My Catholic elementary school made sure we were well-versed on every kind of abortion procedure as if we were surgical interns. No doubt their intention was to ingrain—and traumatize—us into a pro-life stance by forcing their young pupils to watch graphic abortion videos—both early and late trimester. Whether or not we had been given the option to leave the classroom during the videos, none of us left. To leave felt like a game of chicken—to see who could handle the "adult stuff."

No one said anything during our forty-minute lunch breaks, our young minds held hostage by gruesome images. Slices of ham in our otherwise boring little sandwiches suddenly resembled strips of flesh torn apart limb by limb.

As we resumed our regular afternoon session of Social Studies and Science with the expectation that the gruesome images of abortion could be easily forgotten by studying anthropological pictures of the Amazonian peoples, I asked if I could be excused to the bathroom. Most of the girls were starting their periods and we were usually excused without having to explain ourselves. I just needed to be alone. Once excused, I found a classmate already there, crying. When I asked her what was wrong, she snapped, "I hate those videos! My sister had an abortion." I didn't know what to say. My classmate's sister was seventeen.

When we returned to our desks, a classmate boldly raised his hand and asked, "Does this mean it's okay for us to watch *Faces of Death*? It's a documentary from the 70s. You get to see the different ways people die. There's this one scene where they're eating monkey brains!" at which the class exploded in laughter.

"Of course not!" our teacher yelled.

"But you made us watch those abortion videos. *Faces of Death* is just like it except—"

"We're moving on to Math," she replied, cutting him off while the class froze like someone had slammed on the brakes.

As I reflect on that incident thirty years later, the abortion videos did not necessarily scare all of us but held the opposite effect of entertaining our morbid curiosities about death and mutilation.

While the abortion videos focused on the termination of the fetus, which looked more like a froglike humanoid creature, there was never any acknowledgment paid to the faceless woman on the table. I wasn't watching the murder of babies, but rather the grotesque objectification of a woman's body. Surely, women weren't so naïve to undergo such procedures unless for very good reason. The reasons must've been extraordinary, but we were never taught those reasons. The woman on the table wasn't even a woman but simply *spread-legs à la carte*, a mutilated cave of flesh, as we all are if you consider instances of open heart surgery, but my school did not show us videos of open heart surgery.

If my Catholic school believed and taught abortion is murder, then what we were essentially seeing were snuff films. Memories of Catholic school have oftentimes made me wonder what holy means.

School nailed it into our brains that women who have abortions are evil and abortion doctors are evil. They taught us that the need for saving a woman's life over that of a high-risk pregnancy doesn't exist and that pregnancy was one hundred percent safe. They taught that rape rarely resulted in pregnancy since a woman's body goes into shock thereby making pregnancy impossible. They taught us that rape wasn't necessarily evil if it produced a child as they believed God's hand was shining down on the sexual act and blessing it through conception. I see my teacher now — her Catholic hand raised up as if she is God placing her hand over a scene where a man is raping a woman and blessing it with the existence of human life.

The subject of abortion would endlessly follow me as each of these myths would rear its ugly head twenty years later. I'd hear these ridiculous myths preached once again as truth from one such Republican Rep. Todd Akin who would be infamously known for saying that victims of what he called "legitimate rape" rarely get pregnant, stating, "If it's a legitimate rape, the female body has ways to try to shut that whole thing down." Eve Ensler graciously penned her scathing response to shut Akin down, "Did you honestly believe that rape sperm is different than love sperm, that some mysterious religious process occurs and rape sperm self-destructs due to its evil content?" We need not mention the mass rapes of women and girls in war-torn countries, currently and historically, who are impregnated and forced to birth their rapists' children. Or how the tragic death of Savita Halappanavar in Ireland would prove that high-risk pregnancies do exist and can cost women's lives.

But in the days of my Catholic school education, before the internet and social media, my Catholic school would find ways to support their sheltered beliefs through one particular guest speaker whom they would invite back year after year. It was a white female police officer who, on top of preaching that we shouldn't take drugs, also preached that abortion was evil. She told us the story of how she knew a woman who had been raped in a garage by three men who videotaped the rape over three days, and out of that rape, the victim became pregnant. This same officer persuaded her to keep the pregnancy claiming it was God's plan.

I was eleven when I heard this story. I didn't even know what sex was, but the very thought of three men videotaping the rape for three days made me sick and angry. I was undoubtedly angry at the men, but I was also angry at this female officer who told the victim to keep her pregnancy. Deep in my gut, even at eleven, I knew she was wrong. She further taught us how the woman had put her child up for adoption, which the officer praised as the right thing to do, but who knows what happened to that baby? Who knows what happened to the victim?

At recess once again, my classmates had nothing to say. This same guest speaker was invited back several times during 5th, 6th, and 7th Grade. The abortion lessons never ended.

They constantly scared us and racked the girls with guilt that we were nothing but potential murderers if an unwanted pregnancy resulted. How ironic that a decade later, our adult lives would place us in situations where abortion was not a tragedy but charted our lives toward a more favorable course than having us become mothers when we clearly weren't ready.

We were taught to always pray for the election of a Republican president since the Democrats support abortion. The same girl whose older sister had an abortion, this sharp-tongued twelve-year-old, had raised her hand and made the brave observation how we shouldn't vote Republican since "they believe in war and dropping bombs on innocent people." Her observation had been made in reference to the first Bush administration in the Persian Gulf. Iraqi leader Saddam Hussein had then ordered the invasion and occupation of Kuwait in early August 1990. The United States had been called upon to intervene. By mid-January 1991, the Persian Gulf War began with a massive US-led air offensive known as Operation Desert Storm.

"But that's different," my teacher countered. "The soldiers who fight in wars don't hate the other side. God forgives them. They're just doing what they're told. Killing in war just happens. As for people who believe in abortion, they pre-meditatively plan to murder their babies."

"But this war is about oil," another female classmate whose father was a war veteran countered. Rather than further discuss this topic which most of my classmates, including myself, had no clue about the significance of oil in the Middle East, my teacher was clearly stung by both my classmates' counter-arguments and simply cut both girls off. She gave the excuse that we were running short on time and needed to move onto Math. That was my teacher's usual tactic when she had no comeback.

When my best friend and I reminisce about our Catholic school days, the fetus posters and anti-abortion messages don't stand out in our memory. It's only when we see old classroom pictures that we are reminded of the glaring pro-life classroom we sat in everyday, our 8th Grade classroom decorated with fine letters, "ABORTION KILLS CHILDREN," with posters of fetuses as if they were normal school decor. Our collective amnesia over the fetus posters and anti-abortion messages seem to reveal how desensitized we probably became. We only flinch after seeing them thirty years later.

Catholic school classroom, 8th grade, 1991 (photo courtesy of Eliza Gano)

For a long time, I thought abortion videos were part of standard Sex Ed curriculum at all Catholic schools, until adult friends, also former Catholic school students, would gasp in horror when I'd nonchalantly mention the videos as we reminisced and laughed about our zany Catholic school childhoods. Much to my astonishment, we do not share the experience of abortion videos. My Catholic school was rather one of a kind in that respect. I'm not naïve, however, to believe that pro-life lessons such as the ones I grew up with were isolated. They are probably still taught at Catholic and evangelical schools somewhere in this country. Thirty years later, some things never change.

The situation regarding contraception was no different at my Catholic high school. Abstinence was stressed to quiet our raging hormones, and when it wasn't, lessons on contraception were covered in the measly thirty minutes of Sophomore Health class when my teacher hurriedly read aloud from a textbook while many of us had no idea what a condom even looked like. Come graduation, half a dozen girls would be approaching their due dates as they received their diplomas.

With the exclusion of sex education, also came the exclusion of lessons of what a healthy relationship looked like. By the time I had my first boyfriend in college, he made me believe "good" girlfriends had sex, and oftentimes he guilted me into it—what I still have a hard time calling rape. Like any kid of the 90s where the topic of sex was exempt from the household, TV was the main source of information. Rape was a stranger jumping out of the bushes. No one ever said it could be an intimate partner who could unexpectedly turn on you and use sex as a weapon.

When I lost my virginity, it was consensual, even romantic. We were both virgins. How charmed the experience quickly ended. I wasn't on the pill, having believed horror stories that it caused weight gain, acne, painful breast tenderness, and the old wives' tale that it raised the risk of infertility. My boyfriend did not always wear a condom. He practiced the withdrawal method, or so I thought.

I was in my third year of college and on my way to study abroad in New Zealand having earned a highly coveted spot in the study abroad program that year.

They say you know before you know. My period was a week late. As I went on my usual morning run with very sore breasts and overwhelming nausea, I already knew I was pregnant before a campus doctor confirmed it.

I was devastated. I knew I couldn't keep it. My Catholic upbringing, which threatened excommunication and eternal damnation, would not change my mind. Still, I felt the powerful tug of my body's strong instinct to be a mother. It didn't matter that I was nineteen, turning twenty. It didn't matter that I was about to study abroad in New Zealand. It didn't matter that I would face the crushing disappointment of my parents and most likely be forced to marry my abusive boyfriend to save face in my respectable Filipino-American family. My parents had no idea I was even dating anyone. I had never been in a serious relationship before. Distant cousins were already being shipped to the Philippines to hide away the shame of their out-of-wedlock pregnancies. Why not me? I don't think my parents would've gone to that extreme, but who's to say what my father would've done during his disciplinary rage. If my body had had its way, I believe I would've had that baby despite the consequences. But my head knew better. No matter how much I could disagree with my body's instincts, its instincts would eventually hold a small victory over me as the unexpected physiological and mental effects of what I would later understand as trauma would feel like my body's revenge against the rational side of myself.

I confided in my best guy friend about the pregnancy. He was the only other person I told besides my boyfriend. My two best girlfriends were at colleges more than one hundred miles away. I had two sisters, but I didn't feel comfortable confiding in them, at least not then. I had three female roommates, but I kept my pregnancy a secret, sparing myself their judgment and opinions on what I should do. It wasn't anyone's business but mine.

My best guy friend and I were parked outside of his apartment after having lunch together. He was feeding the parking meter when he told me how crappy his week was going. "Not worse than mine," I laughed, adding, "I'm pregnant," at which his jaw dropped.

"What are you going to do? How are you going to continue with school?" he asked, to which I can only guess he assumed I was going to keep it. I nonchalantly responded, "I'm not going to keep it." I didn't bat an eyelash despite the day before, having fled the clinic in tears, running to a secluded spot in the woods, where I rubbed my tummy and quietly told my baby goodbye. I would later place red roses there a few days before my scheduled abortion.

In my eight weeks of pregnancy, I experienced the sore breasts, the stifling nausea, the fatigue, and the hard, muscly shell in my abdomen. I was sad that it was all about to end. I did not go to Planned Parenthood and opted instead for a private clinic of an experienced Ob-Gyn who specialized in first-trimester abortions. I received the referral from the campus doctor. The Ob-Gyn came highly recommended by other college students who had dealt with unwanted pregnancies. A private clinic was more expensive by a couple hundred dollars, which I easily had in my checking account, but more importantly, I wanted to spare myself the stress of facing an angry brigade of pro-life protesters picketing outside Planned Parenthood, which the campus nurse forewarned me about. The private clinic had no such problem.

To this day, the doctor who performed my abortion does not publicly advertise her abortion services. For all the choice, access, and legalization we have in the liberal state of California, the best practitioners can still choose to operate quietly due to fear, safety, and reputation in a predominantly Republican county. My doctor was nothing but compassionate, gentle, and absolutely knowledgeable. I couldn't have had a better doctor. The procedure itself was easy and painless, and took about all of thirty seconds to complete, very unlike the gruesome portrayal in the abortion videos that I was forced to watch during Catholic school.

I was in her office for at most an hour, which included waiting time, consultation, anesthesia prep, the procedure, the pathology report, and recovery. She had two other patients scheduled that afternoon for their prenatal appointments — each woman's round belly bursting with new life. The nurse acted as my doula. She held my hand and provided comforting words while the doctor smoothly performed her magic. Afterward, my boyfriend carried me out of my car and up the stairs into my apartment as I was groggy and nauseous from the anesthesia.

"Don't cry," he commanded while I lay in bed feeling like my heart had been ripped out. How could he tell me not to cry? But I was sad, medicated, and too tired to be angry then. None of my roommates were home. He didn't stay long before he left to study for a Physics exam.

My best guy friend ended up holding me that night. I wouldn't have to grieve alone for the rest of the evening. He didn't hesitate voicing his anger over my boyfriend's abandonment.

"But it's a Physics exam," I explained.

"So what! He should be here!" the friend shook his head.

The friend was right, though I did not speak up and agree at the time.

A few days before, I had gone home to my parents to celebrate my twentieth birthday. I had woken up with a migraine when I heard my mother's familiar call for breakfast. The smell of pancakes wafted into my bedroom which only made me nauseous.

"Sweetheart, are you going to get up? I made pancakes. Why don't you take Tylenol for that migraine?" my mother sweetly said as she sat on the edge of my bed. She kissed the top of my head and held me, simply believing I had a migraine when it was really morning sickness. I silently cried as my mother held me and the quiet grandchild within.

There was no burning desire to tell her. Sex, pregnancy, and dating were never discussed in my household. My pregnancy felt like a grave trespass in their home. There was no alternative but to remain silent. My siblings and I were their academically stellar children who did not make such egregious mistakes. There was a reputation to uphold in our Filipino-American community. I knew I wasn't the only Filipina-American to go through this, but because I told no one, and no one confided their experience to me, besides my classmate's seventeen-year-old sister back in elementary school, I did feel like I was the only one.

A week later, my body returned to normal. I never suffered the uncomfortable cramps and heavy bleeding that is expected. There were soft red swirls and delicate little clumps in the toilet, but outside of that, I bled like I had my period and that was that. My breasts eventually stopped being sore and my abdomen returned to its soft supple self.

During my follow-up exam, the doctor prescribed birth control pills which I unquestionably accepted. In order to get a refill from the campus clinic, I was required to take, for the first time in my life, a comprehensive sexual education class that covered all forms of contraception and sexually transmitted diseases.

Three and a half months later, I was on a plane to New Zealand. No Pinay I knew had ever traveled alone. Traveling alone at twenty as a female, as a Filipina, was daring. For the next nine months, besides my extended family whom I would meet in the Australian Outback, I would encounter only two other Pinays. Outside of that, I would be the only Pinay I knew — in the classroom, my flat, and anywhere in downtown Auckland.

Within the first six months of starting the pill, I switched from an American brand to a New Zealand one when I found that it cost me only $1.50 for a three-month supply versus $30 for what I would've had to pay for the same amount in California. While the American pill lightened my periods, the New Zealand pill made me soak through pads. My naïve self concluded that these body changes must be normal. One can only imagine the dizzying ride my body would endure as it went through a pregnancy, abortion, birth control pill changes, a new country, and a long-distance, abusive relationship all within six months.

The hormones in my body had been constantly fluctuating and I didn't have the faintest idea why. Though depression runs in my family and I suffered occasional bouts during high school, I had never felt as empty as I did in the months following my abortion. The rational side of myself told me that I had done the right thing, but my body and emotions were acting completely opposite. I was taken on a wild rollercoaster ride of sleepless nights and staying in bed all day.

Even though my boyfriend was in California, I remained faithful in a long-distance relationship. He verbally abused me through telephone calls, scoffing at my adventures in a new country, which were then followed by sweet apologetic letters and emails. I thought his jealous behavior was part of a normal relationship despite my gut feeling that something was terribly wrong.

I had wonderful friends, but they still did not have the slightest idea of the emotional turmoil I was under. I feared their judgment and misunderstanding lest I open up about the abuse, and the abortion. On the outside I was charming and unstoppable, while inside, I felt like I was dying.

I disclosed my abortion to two friends in New Zealand, but it was said as a sentence, never a discussion. I remained silent on the subject. My friends were probably too shocked to ask questions. I was the only one I knew who had an abortion in my social circle. I didn't know how to talk about it. I didn't know how to talk about anything then.

That same year, it came to light across the world how forty-nine-year-old President of the United States, Bill Clinton, had had an affair with his White House intern, twenty-two-year-old Monica Lewinsky. She was twenty-four, only four years older than me, when the world found out about their scandalous affair, but at my age, anyone even a few years older felt like decades older. It had not occurred to me how she was merely a kid who had been taken advantage of by a very powerful man who was nearly her father's age and whom the global media unjustifiably painted a slut. I didn't believe she was a slut. I did think she was naïve. The egregiousness of what any of it meant then had not occurred to me. Everyone in every one of my political studies classes had something to say about it, but I had nothing. They asked me what I had thought. Me, the lone Pinay-American in the class. The President of the United States had lied. The President of my country. But I didn't think much about my country. Not then. I had never heard so many twenty-year-olds talk passionately about American politics, yet they surrounded me in Auckland, an entire ocean and hemisphere away. At my college back in Southern California, most college kids talked about parties and drinking and dating. Very rarely did I hear talk about the state of our country or the world.

While Bill and Monica were hot fodder at my New Zealand campus, I could only think of my silence. My abortion. My shame. My anger. My guilt. My classes. My grades. My friends. My boyfriend. My world was very small. Except for my boyfriend, I hardly missed my family and friends in California. I was living, crying, and dying in New Zealand.

Despite weekends lying in bed depressed until 4 PM, I did manage to have an amazing time in New Zealand. I had dared myself to skydive, bungy-jump, hike, run, party, and meet as many people as I could. I had thrown myself into school, studying obsessively and pulling off A's. I was an overachieving superstar, but behind closed doors, I'd retreat to bed in tears before falling asleep. I had become compulsive. I had to keep moving, whether I was studying or socializing or doing some kind of extreme physical activity, while at night, I was allowing myself to cry, to cleanse, to forget. But I never forgot.

At the time, I was unaware that women's bodies had the ability to count down to their due dates. I believe my body counted down to my baby's due date, regardless of whether my mind wanted to or not.

After visiting my relatives in Australia during the winter break, I returned to New Zealand an insomniac and cried for hours every night. I journaled incessantly and wrote long letters about the abortion to my boyfriend, which to a large degree helped me cope with my feelings of isolation. Years later, when I was ready to leave him, he admitted he never read my letters, saying they were too long.

One particular evening, when a friend had fallen asleep in my bed after a late night studying, I was angry inside as her presence interrupted my nightly weeping ritual. She never knew about my ritual, though I made sure no one could ever interrupt it. It was like a drug habit. I believed I needed to cry every night to function normally. I wasn't crying because I missed my pregnancy. I cried because I hated that my stupid self had gotten pregnant and had to go through an abortion in the first place. I hated my boyfriend but believed he could change and understand the pain I was going through. I hated what others might think of me—that I killed my baby, that I was selfish, that I was stupid. And I cried to cleanse myself every night.

I cried night after night until my throat started to hurt beyond the normal sore throat. I visited the campus doctor only to discover that my nightly weeping ritual had developed into tonsillitis. I was terrified that I would require surgery in New Zealand. Luckily, the doctor said it was curable through a simple dose of antibiotics over the next few weeks. If not for the tonsillitis, I might have never realized I was making myself sick. After that, I stopped crying every night.

By the time my twenty-first birthday and first year anniversary of my abortion arrived, I booked a spontaneous weeklong getaway to Fiji alone. It was a cathartic celebration. My mind and body felt more at peace than it ever did since my abortion.

The trauma eventually subsided, but it would take another three years before I was finally ready to leave my abuser. Rather than end the relationship upon my return to California from New Zealand, I made the mistake of introducing him to my parents. I was hopeful that my return would repair our relationship, but things only grew worse as he became more abusive, especially about my academic achievements and career aspirations, accusing me of caring little about our relationship. His attempts to coerce me into sex also escalated to a point where sex lost all meaning and enjoyment. Another year away from him during my first year of law school in New York would help me realize I deserved better.

He never allowed me to talk about the abortion and preferred to call it "a bunch of cells," but would then conveniently bring it up when I tried to leave him. He tried making me feel guilty for leaving by saying we shared the trauma of an abortion together. It was evident we shared nothing about it.

As a Literature major, I would stumble upon Joan Didion's *Play It As It Lays* and Audre Lorde's *Zami*, which helped me make sense of my abortion experience, but what helped me most was becoming a post-abortion counselor. Almost a decade following my abortion is when I finally had the opportunity to grapple with what had happened as I counseled hundreds of women about their abortions.

A part of me still maintains that what I had gone through wasn't that bad. But who am I kidding?

As a post-abortion counselor, I learned that emotional surges following any pregnancy are believed to be a natural effect of the hormone shifts that occur with it. Levels of estrogen and progesterone that increase during pregnancy drop suddenly after childbirth, miscarriage, and abortion. Female hormones are supposed to return to their pre-pregnancy levels within a week or so. As hormone levels normalize, depression that can follow usually resolves on its own without medical treatment. However, factor in poor partner relationships, stress, and a pre-existing history of depression and sexual abuse, and the likelihood of experiencing trauma can be prolonged for more than one year after pregnancy.

I realized how much I had fit into all of the above.

By the time the ten-year anniversary of my abortion arrived, I found myself in a much better place than the decade before. I was starting a new relationship with a kind and compassionate man who would eventually become my husband.

For my thirtieth birthday, I decided to travel without my partner to Hawaii, not only to celebrate my birthday, but to honor my abortion. By then, my partner and I had only been dating six months, and I felt such an occasion seemed only something I could celebrate and fully appreciate.

The idea to travel to Hawaii originated from meeting a Japanese-American filmmaker. I had met her at an art event where we both served as panelists representing the Asian-

American Reproductive Justice Movement. I was there to represent the organization where I volunteered as a post-abortion counselor while she presented her documentary about the Japanese "water baby" ritual of consecrating the spirit of the unformed child to the protection of a Jizo bodhisattva, a "saint" of the Mahayana Buddhist tradition. Jizo is understood to be the protector of those journeying through the physical and spiritual realms. This bodhisattva is closely associated with children, believed to be their guardian before birth, throughout childhood, and after death. As the unborn are seen as beings who float in a watery world awaiting birth, water is thus regarded as the realm where all souls reside before becoming human as well as the realm where the spirit returns.

After seeing her film trailer, I decided to conduct my own investigation of the Jizo before I went to Hawaii, as what better place to be surrounded by water and perform a Jizo ceremony to consecrate the spirit of my pregnancy.

On my thirtieth birthday, my best friend and I launched our kayaks from Lanikai Beach into open water to reach the Mokulua Islands. We had kayaked through giant waves. Our little banana boats bobbed up and down with each swell. I could barely make out my best friend kayaking ahead as a wall of water separated us.

It had been the first time in a long time where it felt like a beautiful homecoming from the abortion and the trauma. I never got to perform the official Jizo water baby ritual in Hawaii, but kayaking in the open water made me feel like I bonded with my pregnancy's spirit in a way that I never had before.

A decade after my abortion, my mother confronted me about my abortion after Googling my name and finding articles I had written. I cannot say she was understanding. My mother was born and raised in the Philippines where abortion is not only considered a mortal sin by its Catholic oligarchy, but is criminal where women brave enough to go through a clandestine abortion risk infertility, infection, even death, if not criminal prosecution and public shaming. I personally knew this to be true after volunteering at a women's health clinic in the Philippines. During a work sabbatical, I took my post-abortion counseling skills to the country of my birth and interned at a post-abortion complications care program, a program specifically created with the purpose of serving women who had clandestinely induced their own abortions and needed emergency, nonjudgmental, post-abortion medical care.

I told my mother that the person who got me pregnant was a rapist. I couldn't tell her it had been the person whom she had welcomed into her home several times. This person whom I called my boyfriend. To her, it could've been a person jumping out of the bushes. It wasn't my intention to protect him but to protect her from further pain in knowing she couldn't protect me.

"I wish I had taught you to avoid it," her voice shook under tears. When my mother cries, it feels as if the ground is splitting and both of our feet threaten to drop off. In my life, I've only seen my mother cry twice. She has always been a gentle and stoic woman. Her words stung as she thought the rape was somehow my fault. I still excused what she said, knowing well that this was, and continues to be, the thinking of the day, that rape is somehow the woman's fault. I never told her, "It wasn't my fault." Instead, I let it go and silently forgave her. I forgave the generation and culture that taught her to think this way about women. I knew my mother wasn't blaming me. She was blaming herself. I simply told her, "It's nothing you could've taught me to stop." We haven't talked about it since.

No matter how many times I write about this experience, I hear the judgment being passed around inside my head. As a Filipina-American, I am walang hiya. I should be ashamed of myself. Whatever trauma I experienced was just punishment for the crime I had committed, when maybe the true crime was being raped and my abusive ex being able to live free from any responsibility and guilt.

My Catholic upbringing had brainwashed me to believe that women who are pro-choice see pregnancy as an unemotional, trivial matter where abortion is a nonchalant decision. It brainwashed me to believe that it is only when women do decide to go through with an abortion that they quickly learn how devastating the experience is and live to regret it, as if the personal experience truly awakens us to the horrors of its psychological damage. It's either that or pro-choice women are self-centered, misguided, reckless, promiscuous, spoiled, and hate children. How untrue all of it was. And yet, how true that the personal experience of abortion didn't awaken me to the horrors of abortion's psychological damage, but awakened me to the psychological damage inflicted by a judgmental society who refuses to trust women's choices.

When the 2012 case of Savita Halappanavar in Ireland made headlines across the world, the pain hit deep. At seventeen weeks pregnant, she died of septicemia a week after being admitted for severe back pain at a Galway hospital where the thirty-one-year-old dentist was told she was miscarrying. She had asked for an abortion several times over a three-day period, during which she was in severe pain, but her requests were denied because a fetal heartbeat was still present. She and her husband were told at one point, "This is a Catholic country." Medical staff removed the dead fetus days later after the heartbeat stopped but Halappanavar died of septicemia.

Savita Halappanavar made global headlines, but how many women like her, nameless and deceased, have demanded an abortion out of emergency medical need and were denied?

As a woman who experienced an anembryonic pregnancy myself, a pregnancy that was very much wanted by me and my husband, it was a dilation and curettage at twelve weeks, a common abortion procedure, that was medically necessary to save me from an unsafe miscarriage, which could have easily resulted in hemorrhaging and infection had I not had the D&C and miscarried on my own. I can attest that the D&C was a quick and clean ten-minute procedure. It was more awkward than painful but nothing like the butchering event that the pro-life movement portrays in their abortion videos.

The abortion videos I was forced to watch at twelve never completely won me over as a pro-life believer. I became pro-choice when I had to make that choice myself, though this is not to say that having an abortion automatically makes you pro-choice, or that being pro-choice means you will remain so. Norma McCorvey for instance, otherwise the Jane Roe of *Roe v. Wade*, had us all believe that she converted to Catholicism twenty years after *Roe*, and had us all believe that she was a staunch pro-life activist until her death, publicly expressing her remorse and denouncing her participation in the case that legalized abortion.

McCorvey stated after becoming pro-life, "I remained basically anonymous for almost seventeen years. I, in those seventeen years, I tried to commit suicide a couple of times. I was very ashamed of what I had done, and I was looking for forgiveness not only from God but from myself."

As of the May 2020 release of Nick Sweeney's documentary, *AKA Jane Roe*, the film shockingly brought to light how McCorvey had in fact supported a woman's choice, but converted to pro-life activism in exchange for money she received from clergy leaders. As she clearly and memorably stated on camera in an ailing condition how this was her deathbed confession: "If a young woman wants to have an abortion, that's no skin off my ass. That's why they call it choice."

If there was anything to learn, McCorvey's deathbed confession in no way should overshadow the compassion felt toward those who do feel remorse following their abortion, and in the case specifically for McCorvey, compassion continues to be felt for many other areas in her life, in what the film revealed as complicated and exploited from both sides of the abortion debate.

Even if McCorvey lied about feeling ashamed for her participation in the groundbreaking Supreme Court case that federally legalized abortion, the subject of shame regarding the abortion experience is still something we pro-choicers need to address rather than shy away from. To shy away from it only seems to fuel pro-life activists, particularly those who have had abortions, into believing that our emotional response is a one-sided narrative of relief, and that we are liars denying that grief and trauma aren't significant, when some attest to feeling these very emotions and nothing else.

As someone raised Catholic, I feel my abortion story makes staunch Catholics believe that I belong in the fiery pit of damnation, expecting me to repent for my mortal sin when my abortion was the only right thing for me to do under the circumstances. I've never felt that I needed to be forgiven by God.

While some may regret their abortions, which may then compel them to reinforce their religious devotion without exception, I hadn't done the opposite to renounce my faith, though I did feel Catholicism had turned its back on me with their rule of *latae sententiae,* automatic excommunication to any woman who has an abortion. My feelings toward the Catholic Church remain lukewarm. I am well aware of the existence of pro-choice Catholics, even the organization Catholics for Choice who advocate on our behalf, but no matter our existence, we remain outsiders to the Vatican who do not see our stance as noteworthy. Church doctrine remains strictly opposed to abortion without exception. It would be naïve to think that Catholic women are ignorant of *latae sententiae* as it is a law deeply ingrained in our catechism. It's important to compare that rapists aren't automatically excommunicated. One need not look further than how the Church handled the sex abuse scandals of their priests, yet we, excommunicated women, are expected to repent to these men whom the Church has bestowed as the only ones capable of officially absolving us of our sins.

The trauma after my abortion only made me fiercely pro-choice, even though a part of me fears the pro-choice community will hate me as I don't necessarily shout my abortion as an empowering experience. To be honest, it was very lonely. Even still, I don't feel totally empowered sharing my abortion story but more than ever feel afraid of judgment and attack from both the pro-life and pro-choice sides.

I firmly believe in the fundamental right to an abortion but also believe trauma can be one of the natural responses to an abortion. I'd like to believe the pro-choice community would welcome me with open arms, but it seems voicing any negative opinions about the abortion experience such as trauma undermines what we're fighting for.

It seems good pro-choicers do not see abortion as a traumatic experience. Good pro-choicers do not see abortion as a tragedy. Good pro-choicers find the abortion experience empowering. Good pro-choicers see abortion as a solution. Good pro-choicers see abortion as a relief. While I agree with the good pro-choicer, I also see what the other side sees and agree with them too.

In 2005, when Hillary Clinton called abortion a tragedy by saying it represents "a sad, even tragic choice to many, many women," pro-choice pundits were quick to voice their skepticism. On a big picture scale, I see why the pro-choice movement swiftly questioned how much of a pro-choicer Clinton truly was. Unfortunately for Clinton as a politician, I understand why it was crucial for her to refrain from such comments as words like "tragic" and "necessary evil" attach a negative connotation when trying to legislatively support abortion. But I can also see that she was speaking from a place so deeply personal and in her own eyes, abortion is a tragedy if solely taken on a personal level and not just a legislative one. The sad thing is how these various feelings toward abortion, whether they be spiritual, celebratory, relieving, remorseful, tragic, or traumatic, have divided us as a movement as if our pro-choice feelings should be a one-size fits all.

I am split down the middle between calling abortion a tragedy and not. Maybe that makes me a bad pro-choicer. But why not be inclusive and leave it to a woman who has gone through an abortion to decide whether she calls her own abortion a tragedy or not, as long as she does not impose that emotion on others.

We can believe we are sparing a child from a future we simply cannot provide for. We can believe we do not want to bring unwanted children into the world. We can still love babies but believe that we ourselves were not meant to be mothers. Besides my own personal experience with abortion, my experience as a post-abortion counselor has proven that different women react differently toward their abortions, whether they came to that decision immediately or through the private counsel of friends, family, their religious community, or alone or after days of serious consideration and reconsideration, with different emotions ranging from relief, sadness, shame, regret, even joy. I've known women who have held ceremonies for their abortions while others have thrown celebrations.

I believe I spared myself and my baby from being terrorized and legally bound to an abuser who would've made my life and my baby's life a living hell. If I had that baby, which a small part of me did want, I believe I still would've been fortunate to finish college with the generous support of my family, but it would've been at the heavy cost of being pressured to marry my abuser to save face in my Filipino-American family versus being a shameful single mother at twenty. I believed my baby deserved better than that. I believed I deserved better than that, and I was able to stop all of it from ever happening.

The pro-life side will argue that I should've considered adoption, but that would've meant having to publicly acknowledge my pregnancy to my family, something that was completely unfathomable. Adoption wouldn't have felt that I alone was giving up my child, but it would've felt like a collective surrender. My entire family would've felt they were giving up the child. I couldn't imagine having to carry my baby for nine months only to have them taken away while I and my family would've spent an entire lifetime mourning and agonizing over whether my child was being treated well or abused or abandoned or feeling resentful of me and us. As someone who has personally worked in adoption and the foster care system, the termination of one's parental rights is far from an easy experience for biological family, biological parents, child, foster parents, and adoptive parents.

Among us pro-choicers, some of us believe abortion is murder, but also believe that our personal well-being and future depend on the life we take. I know saying that is legislatively dangerous and problematic, but personally naming it as such is how some pro-choicers feel and in turn helps particular women and birthing folks grieve, find forgiveness, cope, and move on. To exclude us from the pro-choice conversation only diminishes the many facets and inexplicable complexity of those who identify as pro-choice. At the outset of saying this, I expect harsh criticism from my own pro-choice community, but if we are to shout our abortions, then we need to shout each and every kind. The pro-choice side, though flawed and imperfect and evolving and still arguing on whether we need to change our name or not, still holds room for discussion, even for those who do not choose abortion. Maybe that makes me a bad pro-choicer, but I'm still pro-choice nonetheless.

WHEN THE BODY SPEAKS

Remember the mornings
when maternal ancestors would awaken
and not want to face
the day of a Spaniard
calling them to their quarters

their bodies a physical resource
to master appetites. Anxiety
must've struck their hearts
as they traversed across rice paddies.

The dread that hung
on every footstep
like iron balls
and off they went
with no other option.

Their anxiety morphing
their double helix
to double helix
to me.

How far now
do great-great-great-granddaughters
walk to offices every morning
the weight of their feet
on concrete sidewalks

and the morning wind colliding
against skin and breath

as if it were
the same Brown soft skin
and ancestors' own breath

shuddering
as a white man still claims
our arrival.

For ten years, my husband and I tried for a baby. After several years of trying to conceive naturally and then suffering one miscarriage, we decided to go through six IUI's—the maximum suggested by our fertility specialist before considering IVF. All six failed while I was working as a litigation assistant at a high-end, high-stakes law firm. I didn't have time to use the bathroom and had to rush through a very late lunch at 3 PM.

Both the treatment and my work environment pushed my body to its limits. How did one physically and psychologically demanding experience impact the other? And why did both seem like measures of my worth as a woman? If we break, the story is that we are weak and unworthy to compete in a man's world. But what if this society runs on toxicity masquerading as success? It's the lie we're made to believe our entire lives.

Three years of acupuncture treatments, herbal medicines, invasive medical procedures, and fertility drugs yielded no baby in the end.

THE WORK ENVIRONMENT

As a poet and abortion rights activist, I was naïve about law school and applied at the urging of my pragmatic father, barely got accepted, wanted to drop out the first year, but, again at the urging of my father, miserably pushed myself to a mediocre finish. Upon graduation, nonprofit work was not an option to meet the high cost of living and paying off my loans.

Eight months into my first law firm job, work life was grueling and demoralizing. At twenty-seven, long before pregnancy was an immediate desire, I woke up one morning and realized I didn't have it in me to be a lawyer. Trapped by debt, I reasoned that working as a litigation assistant would keep me financially afloat, put my JD to some use, and give me time to write and do my reproductive rights activism. A litigation assistant position combined the responsibilities of a paralegal, legal secretary, and document reviewer—all in one. It seemed like what the position lacked in prestige, would make up in livability.

As it turned out, I quality-checked and organized tens of thousands of pages of documents for legal discovery and court filings, and researched cases, statutes, and local court rules, while still making sure there was paper in the printer. At four of the six firms throughout my legal career, it was not rare for me to work until midnight or as late as 5 AM, four hours shy of a 24-hour workday. Even a "normal" workday made very little room for lunch breaks and bathroom breaks.

My proven ability to "work in a fast-paced environment" while appearing absolutely Zen in the midst of a fire drill gave the partners the green light to add to my workload. The workload would inevitably become impossible, though I would force it to *be* possible because that's what was expected. I reasoned that my experience could never be as bad as that of a full-fledged attorney.

By thirty, I was not only working a demanding litigation assistant position, but I was a poet, an activist for a Filipina women's organization, a Planned Parenthood volunteer, a post-abortion talkline counselor, and a marathon runner. I was also in a serious relationship with a man who is now my husband. Free time was never free.

I took two unpaid sabbaticals: one to do reproductive rights work in the Philippines, and the other to work on my writing. For two years, I even cut down to a part-time position to complete an MFA in writing. But I always returned to litigation assistant work to cover my loans and the high cost of living in the Bay Area. It seemed like I was living the "work hard, play hard" mantra, which ultimately proved to be the unhealthiest way for me to live.

I moved from firm to firm, anywhere from boutique to mid-size, climbing the pay scale and hoping for a better work environment. The pay improved but the toxicity didn't.

At nineteen, while in an abusive relationship, I became pregnant and ultimately chose to terminate. Almost twenty years later, when I wanted to be a mother, I couldn't get pregnant. Fertility is complex and under-researched. It would be an oversimplification to say that stress prevented me from getting pregnant; after all, it hadn't when I was nineteen. But it certainly wasn't helping matters.

THE FERTILITY JOURNEY

My acupuncturist suggested that quitting my job might be the best way to stop the chronic stress and increase my chances of getting pregnant, but how could I quit when the income was paying for the fertility treatment and even the acupuncture itself?

The medical and wellness communities both agree that when levels of the stress hormone cortisol increase, progesterone levels decrease. Progesterone deficiency is one cause of infertility.

By the time my husband and I were ready to start a family, I learned that I had already aged out of my insurance plan's fertility coverage, which was only available to women under the age of thirty-three. I was never aware there was a cut-off age. If I had known, I am unsure whether my husband and I would've felt compelled to meet the age deadline. I had just started a new job and hadn't accrued much paid time off. I took one unpaid day for each IUI, but those who have gone through it know that the process requires multiple appointments, ultrasounds, and medications throughout your cycle.

I laugh and cringe when people have offhandedly told me, "Don't stress. Then it'll happen." That's like telling a passenger in a falling airplane to not crash.

When compounded with the cost of treatment and the other privileges necessary to conceive, the fertility struggle feels like a further politicization of our bodies, of who is and isn't allowed to have babies. When we talk about reproductive justice, we're usually talking about the right to avoid or end pregnancy. But federal and state legislation and regulations; corporate and insurance company interests; societal expectations; economic infrastructures; and a white supremacist patriarchal culture can manipulate and minimize our chance at childbearing if not totally take it away from us.

For those who want to be pregnant, financial barriers and working conditions can cause us to put off childbearing until much later, when it's more difficult to conceive. A woman's income or lack thereof is tied to her access to abortion. A woman's income or lack thereof is likewise tied to her access to fertility treatment. It should come as no surprise that Black and Brown women are disproportionately affected when it comes to the accessibility of abortion and fertility treatment. Race and class are inextricably tied together in this country, and Black and Brown women have the most to lose when corporate and legislative limitations curtail our reproductive freedom. While this discussion centers cisgender women, nonbinary individuals and transgender men face an added layer of marginalization in their own efforts to access abortion and fertility treatment. Our bodies and our choices, forever tied to the American dollar.

THE INTERSECTIONS BETWEEN WORK, STRESS, AND FERTILITY

Despite western medicine's statistic that women's fertility declines rapidly after the age of thirty-five, I chose to rely on my family history. If my mother, grandmother, great-grandmother, and great-great-grandmother could have healthy babies well into their late thirties and forties, then why not me? But ultimately, I couldn't. I can't fully know the answer to that question, but the weight of urban societal pressures and chronic stress that women face today is very different from the agrarian lives of my maternal ancestors in the Philippines.

During my time as a litigation assistant, I experienced two episodes of proctalgia fugax, which can be induced by chronic stress. I'll let you look up what that is and won't explain it here except all I can say is I experienced it twice, and twice was enough. The pain was so excruciating that fifteen minutes felt like hours.

The first episode occurred while I was at work. I had been sitting at my desk in the middle of a lengthy discovery project when stabbing spasms erupted in a part of my body *anyone* probably hopes never to think about at work. It's an understatement to call them spasms. I thought maybe I needed to use the bathroom, but as I sat in the accessible stall—for some reason thinking I needed a lot of room for whatever I was experiencing—the spasms only intensified. I pulled up my pants and immediately crouched into fetal position in the corner of the stall. If anything, I was glad the bathroom floor of my corporate building was so spick-and-span that it seemed okay to completely crumple onto the tile in my business slacks and fancy heeled boots. Had my great-great-grandmother ever found herself crouched in fetal position suffering stabbing spasms, worried about a 5 PM deadline?

I took deep breaths and started to imagine myself calling an ambulance. There were two other stalls in the women's bathroom, but I was all alone. I could not help crying as I crushed my knees to my chest praying the pain would go away. I imagined the ambulance making their way, stretcher and all, to the twelfth floor, making such a scene that it all dissolved in my head out of shame before anything could materialize.

I took more deep breaths for a few minutes and then rose from the floor. I debated whether I should go home. I washed my hands and looked at myself in the mirror. I knew very well I couldn't just drop everything. A tsunami of legal discovery had to be served by the end of the day.

I straightened my outfit and slowly walked down the hallway when the pain had subsided. I approached my desk cautiously and sat down very gently—in a way where I wasn't putting complete weight on the area where the stabbing pains had originated. The rest of the day, I made no sudden movements of any kind, and took several deep breaths. No one noticed the physical turmoil I was experiencing. Luckily, I was able to serve my discovery and finished the day without further incident.

When it happened again two days later, waking me in the middle of the night, I lay in bed Googling, trying to figure out what the hell was wrong with me. I didn't bother waking my husband. What could he have done except stay up with me and worry?

When I told my husband the next day about what had happened at work and in the middle of the night, we both agreed the stress of the job had reached fever pitch, that everything about the work I had been doing for so long was finally and literally ripping my insides apart.

During this same time, I had just gone through my fifth failed IUI.

THE NEED TO DISMANTLE WHITE SUPREMACY IN THE WORKPLACE

Since I quit my job, I haven't suffered another episode of proctalgia fugax. My periods are healthier, even without acupuncture and other medical treatments. If not for infertility, my periods speak to me as a marker for my general health. While working at the firm, I tried to force my uterus to be healthy, but I was in an environment that was actively hostile to the hypothetical baby's mother. My body would never be safe to house a baby.

I now sleep, eat, and rest well, more than I ever did in my almost twenty-year career. I no longer rush myself to do anything. I currently have long discussions with friends about white supremacy in the workplace regardless of what industry we're in. We never named it before.

By white supremacy in the workplace, I'm referring to what American grassroots organizer-scholars Tema Okun and Kenneth Jones describe as a culture—one which underpins professionalism today—where "objectivity" is hyper-valued; urgency and quantity are paramount to quality; perfectionism leaves little room for mistakes; and certain styles of dress and speech are centered. In this environment, traditional values from Black and Brown cultures are dismissed.

In an American society that glorifies work but undervalues the worker to the point of physical and mental exhaustion (not to mention the denial of benefits for millions of workers), rest and self-care are downplayed as laziness and self-indulgence. I am a Brown Asian woman and daughter of immigrants, with high expectations from my own parents to succeed in an industry that remains overwhelmingly white and privileged.

Despite all the praise about my work at all of the law firms I have ever worked at, I never felt supported unless I *demanded* it, which is emotionally taxing in itself. The responsibility for a livable working environment falls on the worker. And those in authority wonder why the "good ones" always leave.

One story: An attorney, Latina, early thirties, fresh from maternity leave, was not offered a break during a long client meeting to breast pump. She had to sit for five hours straight, risking mastitis and breast engorgement. When she voiced how she was unable to breast pump or even eat lunch due to the managing partner's failure to call for a break, she was told, "You should've just said something." As if the meeting were easy to interrupt.

A second story: An attorney, Asian, late twenties, had worked up to the last possible hour during labor *at the firm* before she rushed herself to the hospital to deliver her baby. She was applauded the next morning for her hard work and determination, with little acknowledgment given to her health, well-being, and even that of her baby.

A third story: An attorney, white, late twenties, had arrived at the office one morning and, after an hour, decided she needed to go home. No one at the time knew she was pregnant and was suffering morning sickness. When the partner found out how abruptly she had left to go home even after it was explained she wasn't feeling well, he was upset she would "just drop everything like that."

A final story: Me, a litigation assistant, Filipina, late thirties, had just suffered a miscarriage. I took two weeks off to recover. My boss, a white woman, agreed to the weeks off but tried to find out more information about my miscarriage from coworkers and even my husband when I told her I didn't want to discuss it. When I returned to work, the office manager had resigned for a better work opportunity. My boss wanted me to take on the office manager's role on top of my litigation assistant responsibilities. I told her she would need to hire an office manager and I wouldn't do it regardless of her offer of a pay increase. She determined the office manager job could be easily combined with my workload, which she determined was not heavy. I resigned a month later.

A white supremacist work culture conspires against pregnant women, women trying to conceive, and new mothers in an industry that society perceives as prestigious. All the women mentioned above were not law partners. With the exception of one or two men of color in the highest position as partners, the partners of the firms I have worked at were always white men and white women.

I do not come from a family of lawyers. I do not come from money. I come from two hardworking parents who encouraged me to earn the best education so I could have "all the things." It was a well-meaning lie. It's such an understatement to say, "We tried to have a baby, but it just didn't happen."

Gone now are the days of periods mucky and brown. In fertility speak, you cannot successfully plant in dry, cracked soil and expect anything to grow. All the fertility drugs in the world could not defy what Mother Nature was trying to tell me.

It seems unfair to gauge my life as less stressful without children when an unbearable workload contributed to making it impossible for me to conceive in the first place. One cannot downplay the toxic effects on the body happening in the workplace. Your body will tell you when something is wrong. And you need to listen.

EDGE

Naim-imbág ti matáy ta malipátanen ngem ti agbiág a
maibabaín.
It is better to be dead and forgotten than to live in shame.

*Thirteen-year-old Filipina-American Izabel Laxamana jumped off of
a bridge in Tacoma, Washington, on May 29, 2015. She died on May
30 from her injuries. On May 27, a video posted on YouTube had
shown Izabel standing next to a pile of her hair, which her father had
cut as a form of punishment for sending suggestive photos to a boy.
The video garnered four million hits within two days. Police claim
that according to suicide notes left by Izabel, the public shaming
video had nothing to do with her suicide and thus charges were not
filed against her father.*

The first time: the edge of a coat hanger. An old metal one. The
one I imagined women used before *Roe*. The edge usually
curled around the bar in your closet, holding the weight of a
dress, a pair of jeans, a jacket.

I straightened the curl, slashed the tip against the inside of my
forearm, the skin thin and soft. A smooth pink path was lifted
across. Hundreds of tiny red dots rushed to the surface and
didn't break through. The pointy edge wasn't very sharp. I
had to push hard, even then, a moment of hesitation, stopping
myself from teetering too close to the edge.

The pink raised path along my arm was enough.

This time: the hanger.

Next time: blunt objects like dulled scissors. Never sharp enough to prick skin, but dull enough to ride the inside of my arm like a bumpy dirt road, leaving its tracks in the sand.

I always stopped myself out of:
- fear of falling too fast without having the heart to change my mind—
- hope tomorrow will be better—
- pagbabalik—

We sit for the longest time, straddling the fence.

Ms. Izabel Laxamana. Your beautiful long hair. Your smile could be my sister's. Your smile could be my own.

You who didn't need much to grow into her own.

I wanted so deeply to hold your hand. Bumalík ka sa akin.

I would've whispered to you. Agsublí ca caniác.

I would've pleaded. *You are going to get through this.*

But I wasn't there. I only heard of your fall. Of you meeting relief.

Release.

Does your community think you a coward? Blame you for not taking life's knocks?

> Ukininam. Fucking stupid.
> Anak ni diablo.
> Fucking gago.
> Our folks making rhymes.
> To sing us to sleep.
> To tear us apart.

The consequences of getting messed up, man, you lost all that beautiful hair, a male voice can be heard saying from behind the camera. The video pans down. Your long locks of black hair are scattered on the ground. *Was it worth it?*

> *No,* you respond flatly.

> *How many times did I warn you?* he asks.

The popular but hush-hush solution had been sending us to Ináng-bayan to discipline us, banish us, teach us the ultimate lesson, *I can't deal with you right now.* Parents deport us even when we have never ventured across the Pacific to the land of our ancestors. Parents cut us off from the only home we have ever known. And if not that, your father cuts off your hair from your Diasporic body of rebellion and flirting and leaves you with one lock of long hair to remind you—not so much what you had lost but—what he could still take.

I know your father's voice. Your *No* resonates through my body, when I would've stood silent, too afraid to speak.

You are fucking stupid.

—That was my father's twenty-five years before your YouTube video posted.

How many times?
How many times?
How many times?
How many times?
How many fucking times?

The reasons are endless but are they ever enough?

I've seen those reasons lead me to that bumpy blood-road on my arm, leaving its tracks, or you with your second leg making the final leap to the other side, the memory of your cut hair already a fallen veil.

This is not a contest you or I want to ever win.

Let's stop this, please.
Bumalík ka sa akin.
Agsublí ca caniác.

Izabel.
Izzy.
Baby Girl.
Balasang co.

Breath.
Pause.
Deep breath in.

GIVING BIRTH IN A TIME OF WAR

A week before Valentine's Day, my mother was conceived as Japan and America and the Philippines bombed each other in communion.

Shortly after, my mother's father, not even Lola's husband yet, had gone underground, a guerilla, uncertain of his return. Lola would run across fields, dodging bombs while clutching the hem of her malong, and my mother inside Lola's full belly would be rocked to sleep by the lulling motion of knees galloping and bare feet stampeding as Lola ran into hiding from Japanese soldiers.

After the bombings, she and her in-laws would emerge and catch a blood-orange sun behind an ashen fog of bomb wisps and shell droppings like flittering snow. Her beautiful tresses catching dust and gunpowder flakes.

This was how the world fell apart.

Hospitals had been bombed, and so Lola had given birth at home—her husband's home—I cannot remember what she told me, though I was already inside my mother's egg.

My mother did not slide out easily as Lola clenched her fists, dripping feathers and sweat with ropes of cloth tied to the corners of the bed. She never forgot the pain (though women are otherwise told) and never forgot the restless knocking of the bamboo fountain outside. Each little bucket filled and then toppled and released, knocking wood against wood endlessly through the night.

My mother's newborn screams would mirror the rhythmic knocking of wood against wood, her tiny body a conduit for the spirits of her aunts and uncles who had been murdered earlier that week. They whose spirits echoed in the knocking of wood against wood. They who had been hung by their ankles from the trees.

They must have just arrived inside the warm blue light, only to be pulled back from the depths through their niece's newborn cries, experiencing War. All. Over. Again. They would be she and she would be they, except her newborn self would bewitch Japanese hearts with her baby eyes / baby cheeks / baby giggles. They would not toss her delicate little body into the air and catch her on their bayonets. Instead, they would tickle her cheeks and coo, *Such a pretty baby.*

Her aunts with their long temptress tresses could not bewitch as their newborn niece had done.

Hung by their slender ankles from the trees, their hair would cascade onyx waterfalls until their souls would finally make their escape into hers, into mine —

Loly Fely, circa 1940

STONE

*In the Ilocano tradition, a "dung-aw" is a poetic wailing for the dead;
a dirge. At a funeral, a dung-aw would be performed by a family
member — as messages to be carried to the afterlife, as a way of asking
forgiveness, or expressing gratitude to the deceased loved one. The
dung-aw is a mystical ritual showing respect. Here, the dung-aw is
an incantation, a conjuring.*

My mother never met her father. She was four-months-old
when he died. I was nine-years-old when I first learned his
name.

My school assignment was to create a family tree. I had
to ask my mother her father's name. My mother had never
talked about him. I first learned about him through my
father's sister who mentioned how he had died a soldier
during World War II, but that was the only story I'd know. My
mother would remain silent, not offering any stories about her
father to her young children.

My mother was picking green beans in our backyard
while holding a large silver bowl. It had been a couple of
hours before dinner, the sun splashing a deep orange across
her face and hands.

I dove in. Not courageously, but to get it over with.
"What was grandpa's name?"

"You mean, my dad?" Her voice shook. A glassy sheet
fell over her eyes as she quickly reached for a green bean.

"Dominador."

I ran back inside and misspelled his name: D-O-M-I-N-I-D-O-R.

At dinner, she was unusually quiet. I had asked the question I was never supposed to ask. I had forced her to think of her father, a man whom I believed she rarely thought of. Now we were both thinking of him.

Since then, it had always been difficult to approach my mother about her father. The same shakiness in her voice and glassiness in her eyes would always surface.

At twenty-six, during my grandmother's last visit from the Philippines, I lay next to my grandmother on our guest room's baby blue embroidered quilt. She was lying down with rosary in hand, her way of evening meditation, relaxing into a trance as she muttered Hail Mary's repetitively.

"Praying again?" I asked. I was eleven all over again, when Lola Fely and I had shared a room.

"Of course. You are the only grandchild who talks to me," she smiled.

Stories were buried in her body. I wanted them.

Lola Fely had smooth Oil of Olay cheekbones, and her jawline caved in as she refused to wear her bottom dentures. They hurt her too much. They had never fit quite right. She'd pull her lips in and smell your cheeks, inhaling you deep into her lungs—the infamous Lola Fely sniff kiss, taking in the full scent of you.

When I was five, she scolded her grandchildren if we ever called her, "Lola Itas," a moniker of her full name, Felicitas. She preferred instead the nickname, "Lola Fely." Now, retired for twenty years after a four-decades long career as a schoolteacher, she derisively recalled the nickname her co-teachers had given her: "Citas," which sounded even more unfitting than "Itas." At eighty-four with twinkling eyes and perfectly smooth cheekbones, Lola Fely now giggled like a schoolgirl, radiating her usual gentle magnetism as we laughed over how ironically infelicitous her old nicknames had been.

At twenty-six, it doesn't occur to me that in four-and-a-half years I will lose Lola Fely to senility. She will still be beautiful with dark brown wavy hair and smooth tan skin, dressed in an elegant floral silk duster, but she will not know who I am when I at thirty-one will surprisingly show up on her doorstep in Cubao, throwing my arms around her in excitement while she will scowl at me in return, as if I were her long lost enemy. I'm still at the spoiled age when I think Lola will never lose her memory. I'm still at the spoiled age when I think Lola will always be fluent in three languages. I'm still at the spoiled age when I think we can always share stories, laugh uproariously, and have serious conversations. I'm still at the spoiled age when I think we will never become strangers. I'm still at the spoiled age when I think Lola will live forever.

Her home was the Philippines. Her visit felt like my last chance to know her, to know about her husband, my grandfather. I did not know when I would see her again. I asked her questions about who she was, and I asked the question that baffled me all my life: *how exactly did her husband die.* I wanted details. Not the usual, "Oh, he died fighting the Japanese during World War II." All Filipinos seemed to have their fair share of war stories, collecting bits and pieces of information from grandmothers, grandfathers, great aunts, great uncles, not suffering from dementia, Alzheimer's, or shame.

"A Filipino killed him," Lola Fely answered, as if answering a simple mathematical equation.

"What?" A cannonball had been blown through my stomach.

"A Filipino killed him. Your Lolo was a rifleman, but he was ordered to fight with the machine gun unit, and he didn't want to fight with the machine gun unit. He didn't know how to fight with a machine gun. They killed him over that. That's what the messenger told me."

"I thought he died during the Death March. I thought the Japanese murdered him."

"He survived the Death March. The Japanese murdered his father. They came to the house looking for your grandfather. They knew he was a guerilla and came to the house often. During one of their visits, they stomped on his father's chest and hung his brothers and sisters to the trees. My husband and father-in-law died within a week of each other. But your grandfather, it was a Filipino. A Filipino killed him."

"But why?"

"Because there are bad Filipinos too," she replied, as if her answer was what I already should've known. *Because there are bad Filipinos too.* We were Kababayan. All of us. The Spanish could cut us down. The Japanese. The Americans. Even our government. But not Kababayan.

Because there are bad Filipinos too.

World War II stories concerning Filipinos were always steeped in brotherhood. No one ever shared stories about their Lolos being murdered or betrayed by their fellow men. It was unheard of. We were taught that Filipino soldiers supported each other, fought for each other, and were still fighting together for their much-deserved compensation for having served under the United States Army during World War II.

Because there are bad Filipinos too. Her words resonated like an awful lullaby.

"We went to the place where they killed and buried him. Your mother was a little girl by the time his brothers and cousins exhumed his bones so he could be brought home to be buried."

"Did you see his face? Did you see his body? Are you sure it was him?"

She said she didn't need to see his face, but she confirmed that he wrote his last message on a stone. The stone had marked where they buried him. It said,

March 5, 1945
Fely, this is where I died bravely.
Doming

She glided her index finger across the air as if scrawling the message the way Lolo would've done.

"Where is this stone?"

"Your Lola Ising chiseled the message out and brought it to her house. It was originally on a much bigger stone. She cut out the part where the message was written." She gestured with her hands what a small part was. "It's underneath the stairs in her house."

I remembered Lola Ising's house in La Union. Lola Ising, Lolo's eldest childless sister who, sitting beside me on her bench when I was ten, had pulled up my left pant leg to see my skin, and laughed, "You have sweet American blood. That's why the mosquitoes like you."

Lola Ising, age 78, with me, 10 (left) and my sister, 8 (right),
Ubbog, La Union, 1988

"Is it still there?" I asked my grandmother.

"I haven't seen it for a long time," she laughed. It wasn't a real laugh, but an instinctive reply in place of a sigh. Bahala na.

When I was ten, my family had gone to stay with Lola Ising for a few days in the summer. My mother and her aunt had been very close, closer than what her relationship might've been with her own mother, that each regarded one another as adoptive mother and adopted daughter.

That summer, I ran around Lola Ising's house; spent lazy afternoons in her sala; played with her basket of gray kittens in the kitchen; fed chichacorn to her curly-tailed guard dog, Boomer, a butterscotch-faced Akita; and amusingly watched her cow from the upstairs verandah relieve itself in the brown, wild meadow with large heaps of dung. It was the same verandah where Lola Ising had shushed my mother's infant cries after her father died and after her mother left for Manila to finish college and establish her teaching career.

In an 11x14 sepia photograph framed in Lola Ising's living room, my twenty-year-old Lolo stood at-ease in his army uniform and knee-high boots, with his name signed underneath: Dominador Corpuz Orejudos. It was then I realized I had been spelling Lolo's name wrong since that family tree assignment.

First Lt. Dominador Corpuz Orejudos, circa 1940 (the bottom of the original photograph bearing his signature had been cropped out to fit Lola Fely's 8x10 frame)

When I eventually asked my mother about her father's stone, she froze with downcast eyes and muttered quickly, "The stone? I know about the stone." When I asked what she knew about her father's death, she confirmed the details in whispers as if his executioners would somehow rise like duende from the dirt. She was ashamed to tell me. She was ashamed that I knew. I wanted to tell her, "It wasn't his fault," but my mother is the kind of woman who believes that victims are somehow at fault, as if the victim could've stopped it. I didn't know how to tell her that that's not how it works.

In a voice so low, she confirmed, "See, *what* it is, is that Auntie Ising, all of us, we knew who the informant was, the one who squealed on my dad to the Japanese that my dad had joined the guerillas. The informant lived in our neighborhood. We knew exactly who it was. The informant had been a Japanese collaborator, and when the Japanese found out about my dad, the soldiers came and hung three of my aunts upside down and trampled my grandfather. The Japanese tortured them. My grandfather, Alejo, didn't make it."

There is a clamoring omission from my mother's account of what the Japanese soldiers might have further done. Of what they *did*. There is only the juxtaposition of words, of what was told to her by her mother and aunts who survived the War. *Japanese soldiers | Aunts | Torture | Trees.*

Stories of comfort women reemerge into my consciousness from books and documentaries and interviews — stories of young Pinays and their chance encounters with Japanese soldiers, covering themselves in mud for a reason; stories from my Pinay friends whose Lolas told their own survival stories to their granddaughters about the War.

I don't ask my mother for details. The words — Japanese soldiers | Aunts | Torture | Trees — are enough.

My infant mother was the daughter of a wanted guerilla. They would've killed her. They would've tossed her up into the air and caught her infant self on their bayonet. But her fat cheeks reminded a soldier of his daughter or granddaughter back home in Japan. They simply tickled her cheeks as her mother and aunts watched with bated breath. My mother's infant cuteness had the power to turn a Japanese soldier's heart into putty in her tiny infant hands. She was a mystical baby who despite being born into madness would not be swallowed by it.

"My dad didn't die by the Japanese. He survived the Death March and still joined the guerillas. A guerilla commander killed him because my dad disobeyed him, accused him of insubordination. Can you believe that? Insubordination when my dad was a First Lieutenant who survived the Death March. My dad just didn't agree with him. My dad didn't believe that the orders he was given were right and he was killed over that."

"Insubordination" was the reason given. But it wasn't *the* reason. No one was supposed to know a Filipino killed him, as if knowing this fact made her father less heroic because he wasn't killed by the Japanese enemy.

Kababayan are not supposed to kill each other. That is the rule. But we do.

And her father *was* at fault. For leaving behind his one and only child.

The stone had sat somewhere in that house, a hidden pile of gold with Lolo's handwriting, while his ten-year-old granddaughter had run around his sister's house unaware of its existence. My mother and great aunt never peeped one word of it. Their silence carried a wound so deep that I could not comprehend how it still bled for my mother who never had the opportunity to call her father, "Pa," as she called her mother, "Ma." The wound carried a tired bitter rage that risked fully consuming a person and maybe that long-held silence was its way of prohibiting that rage from consuming you or you'd hate your own goddamn self—your Filipino self and skinship.

My mother would remember her mango tree and the sarguelas tree located near the stone, positioned by the front post of the house. The mango tree was hers, planted by her father, thus it was named *her* tree, while she would describe the sarguelas tree in detail—its leaves, the taste and texture of its fruit, the way it reclined near the stone like a languid goddess.

There would be no photograph of the stone. Only memory. Forces of wind, rain, humidity, and sun would ultimately wither away any evidence of her father's last message.

First Dung-aw

I, an old Ilocana espiritista, conjure you, hoist you up from March 5, 1945—the day someone told you to get down on your knees. And pray.

What were your big ideas? Would I have even liked you? Were you a nice guy?

Your surviving Brown brothers line the blank skinny margins in American high school textbooks as a white government smirks, and your Brown brothers dissolve one by one in their faded army uniforms and empty pockets. And yet here I am in America, living inside the irony: I am here You are dead.

America—the country that you served only to have your blood on their hands.

Is this the freedom you wanted—God, education, capitalism, success—or did you change your mind when the bullets hailed down?

Your grandchildren live in the Kanong Halimaw and swallow the Kano Dream like Kronos who swallowed his children whole until the Dream would be severed from their heads and tumble out of their minds.

We leaf through textbooks silencing your name, not considered a blonde-hair blue-eyed boy's history, where Mac-Ar-thur is so much easier to pronounce than Ore-ju-dos—the J pronounced a capital H as in Hello Hell Hate Heathen.

I had hoped it wasn't you, that your beloved Fely was simply mistaken into believing it was you as she never saw your face even after your Bacnotan brothers exhumed your bones from your shallow beach grave.

Your wife would properly deliver you into the womb of Pilipinas, in the gentle way you should've been laid to rest, after your Brown brothers took your life for shady reasons, except you must've been a threat with your grand guerilla ideas for your Pilipinas to be free. Free from Japan. Possibly even from America.

You were Fely's husband / cousin / uncle. Like Antigone who sought to bury Polynices murdered by their own brother, Eteocles, you too were killed by your own brothers—your Kababayan—only to have your Antigone reclaim your bones and bring you home.

I had always thought the Japanese murdered you. It was Our war against them, until your wife revealed fifty-nine years after your death that it was a guerilla commander who killed you over a petty disagreement—you and your unit were ordered to use machine guns. You argued being an expert at rifles.

They killed you over that, First Lieutenant Orejudos, simply over that.

Enemy then flipped from the Japanese to the Amerikanos to the Filipinos to our people to our families to you to me.

After sixty years of silence, your wife and daughter simply accept there are bad bad people in the world not worthy of mention. Their silence drapes the hard truth of Brown brothers dispensing their own.

We forget the dirty details of how Diego Silang died under his own brother's hands while Brown children are taught to believe in the American Dream, Santa Claus, and other fairy tales.

We blame Spain. We blame Japan. We blame the United States, when your wife and daughter tell me quietly who it was, truly, who held the guns.

I see you, My Caesar, turning to your brothers before you fall, *Et tu Filipino?*

A young-old ghost, a body of only twenty-eight years. I want to believe in brotherhood when the truth of your death shatters these Filipino-American dreams.

We are liars.

Your hands, air. Your hair, dust. Your lips, a soft icy brush against my hair, my cheeks.

The sweet scent of your sweat and dried streams of your blood swirl like ribbons, only to unravel a wild Ilocana espiritista waking inside your American granddaughter's bones.

At thirty-one, I returned to the Philippines, taking a four-month sabbatical to volunteer at a Filipina women's health organization in Quezon City. The last time I had been in the Philippines, I was ten for a summer vacation, and before that, I was sixteen-months-old before we ultimately immigrated to California.

"Don't get yourself killed. They kill people who want to help others. You'll see, balasang, they will try to cut you down," my father warned, a toothpick hanging from his lips as he continued his game of solitaire, his cards neatly laid out on the sofa.

I am my Lolo's granddaughter.

Equipped with a list of contacts my mother had given me, I made my first contact with one of my maternal relatives after a business trip to Bulacan where I had been assigned to visit barangay hospitals.

In Bulacan, I met up with my cousin, Romar, who was a year older than me and lived in the neighboring province, Pampanga. Our Lolos, Dominador and Amadeo, were brothers, thus our mothers were first cousins. Romar drove me to his home in Pampanga which was an hour away and where I was to spend four days.

Romar was handsome, almost six feet tall, lean with tan skin and jet-black hair.

"Wow! You're a real good-looking guy!" I said when we first met. Romar was taken aback by my remark and laughed while blushing.

"You'd call me Manong," he said.

"You're a year older than me. Is it okay if I don't?"

"That's okay," he said, excusing my American rudeness.

As we drove from Bulacan to Pampanga, we passed countless Iglesia ni Cristo churches which resembled Mormon temples back in California. They loomed large and out-of-place among the small, simple towns we passed.

"These Iglesia ni Cristo churches are everywhere!"

"I should tell you, our family belongs to Iglesia ni Cristo," Romar said.

Why didn't my mother tell me? I thought.

"Oh," I said, embarrassed, stopping myself short from adding that I thought all their churches looked like the Disneyland castle.

"Would you like to come to a service with our family on Sunday?"

"I'm Catholic," I said. I wasn't a practicing Catholic, but it was my excuse to avoid going to their church.

"We still have Catholics in our family and there are no hard feelings between us."

When we arrived at his house, a large part of the Orejudos clan resided with him, about fifteen of them in an unfinished three-story mansion located in a gated housing development, popular among retired Balikbayans whose dream had been to return to the Philippines after having spent their lives in the United States.

The floors were cement with no carpet, tiles, or hardwood floors. The air conditioner was turned up so high that I felt I needed a sweater despite the humid ninety-degree weather outside. All electrical wiring was exposed on the ceiling. I thought the house was in the midst of a temporary renovation, but Romar revealed how its status of disrepair had been like that for three years. "I don't know when we'll ever get it done. We don't have the money to finish it."

The only room that had been finished was the upstairs bathroom with pink flowered tiles, a shining ceramic sink and a flushing toilet, though they still did not have hot water.

Romar, his wife, and four-year-old daughter lived on the third floor. It was a private one-and-a-half bedroom apartment that had its own kitchen, bathroom, and balcony. Their yaya occupied a very small living space to the right of their living room.

As Romar and I stood on his balcony and viewed the rest of the housing development down below in the cool evening air, Romar told me, "I want to go to America. I feel like if I worked like a carabao, at least I'd get rich in America. But here, you work like a carabao, you die like a carabao. It's never easy. We are okay with my job, but in this country, you just never know if it will be gone. There could be another people's revolution and then everything you worked hard for is just gone, and you'd still be a carabao. Everyone has money in America. Yes?"

"There are homeless people in America."

"But I never see them on TV."

"They're always going to show you the rich, beautiful, and famous on TV. They won't show you the homeless."

During that weekend, it was Romar's idea to bring me to Bataan, where Lolo had fought and where the Death March trail began.

As we ascended Mt. Samat in Romar's Range Rover, it had begun to rain amid surrounding hills that appeared smoky and dreamlike. The jungle flora drowned everything in an ocean of dark green tendrils everywhere. Despite its lush landscape, there were no resorts or development here. The area had very much remained unchanged since the War. Sightings of ghosts of fallen soldiers ran rampant. Romar told me how no one dared to camp here. The higher we went, I imagined Lolo very far from home—almost five provinces away from La Union. He and his unit must've traveled by foot through the dense jungles down the western coast.

Our destination was Dambana ng Kagitingan, a "Shrine of Valor" that featured a 90 meter-high crossbar with battle scenes carved around its base, displaying heroes such as Jose Rizal, Padre Burgos, and Emilio Aguinaldo. Ferdinand Marcos had the shrine constructed for the 25th Anniversary of World War II.

We took the elevator up to the crossbar. A viewing gallery overlooked Mt. Mariveles, Manila Bay, the South China Sea, and a hazy view of Corregidor Island. Lolo had escaped death in these very hills. The entire landscape was enveloped in an eerie fog. The blood of tens of thousands of fallen soldiers had intermingled with the soil, long nurturing the lush landscape of green tendrils below. Their last breaths eternally exhaled from the trees and leaves and wind and raindrops that now kissed our faces as we peered out of the open windows. We could feel the wind push against the crossbar so there was a swaying motion as you walked across the viewing gallery. Romar was terribly afraid of heights and sat on the floor next to the elevator.

As we hiked our way down to the open-air chapel featuring a dazzling multi-colored mosaic, Romar told me, "When we brought Lola Ising here, she cried. It was very emotional for her." I imagined Lola Ising, Lolo's eldest sister, an old woman, hunched forward, shawl around her, tears rolling down her cheeks, quietly wailing her dung-aw.

Memories of her brother, the Japanese, and the War must have flooded ghosts through her entire frame.

For the rest of the afternoon, Romar drove us down a portion of the Death March trail. Kilometer markers had been posted on the main road, featuring the faceless and shadowed figures of two men hunched over, both their heads bowed, one walking behind the other with shoulders forward and slack arms while the man in front crawls on his hands and knees. I had trouble processing the fact that I had been on the actual trail Lolo marched on and survived.

On our drive back to Pampanga, Romar and I discussed how Lolo had died.

"I heard he was stabbed to death," Romar said.

"I always thought he had been shot." I stepped back from that statement and thought about it. It was an easy assumption when Lola Fely never told me he was shot.

Romar's own maternal grandfather, Lolo's brother, Amadeo, had also been murdered by Kababayan in 1972. Amadeo was a barangay captain who was found beheaded after he went up to the mountains to gather firewood. The motivations of his detractors were unclear though seemed political in nature considering Amadeo's position as barangay captain. Had Amadeo been outspoken, progressive, a revolutionary like his big brother?

As my father warned me before I embarked on my sabbatical as a women's reproductive health intern, "Don't get yourself killed. They kill people who want to help others. You'll see, balasang, they will try to cut you down."

I am my Lolo's granddaughter.

Romar added, "Your Lolo was an Iglesian."

I was shocked as my mother and Lola Fely were devout Catholics. I never would've guessed Lolo was Iglesian. However, to learn he wasn't Catholic when the rest of the country was, revealed so much about him as a revolutionary at the time. Spain had eradicated our Babaylan spirituality and swept the entire archipelago for nearly four hundred years with Catholicism. Iglesia ni Cristo was a new religious movement founded by a Filipino, Felix Manalo, in 1914, what would have already been a time when the Philippines was still recovering from three hundred and seventy-seven years of Spanish colonial rule and acclimating to the beginning of American colonial rule.

It seems Lolo was not just a rebel in war but religion.

I couldn't help but notice the eerily similar fates between Dominador and Amadeo, the only two brothers who shared their father's Iglesian faith. Both brothers rose as leaders but were murdered by their own men, leaving grandchildren in their wake who would know little of their patriarchs. We would gather up pieces of information like scattered bits of glass. We would never know all the answers.

When Sunday arrived, Romar insisted I attend an Iglesia ni Cristo service, possibly as a way of connecting me to the religion of our maternal grandfathers.

Since I didn't have proper church attire packed for that weekend, bringing only mini denim skirts, shorts, and tank tops, Romar's wife lent me a few dresses to choose from. My choice was based on what was the least frumpy. It was a difficult decision. What I ultimately chose was a pink floral dress that hung on me like a drape down to my calves. She lent me white flats to match.

"Wow!" Romar's four-year-old daughter said, gazing at me as if I were a life-sized Maria Clara doll.

Their church looked like another Disneyland castle, except much bigger than the ones we passed in Bulacan. I was told to follow the wife of one of my cousins inside. Romar and his wife were part of the Church choir, all robed in white and seated in a front balcony, separated by gender. On the left side of the church, men were seated, and on the right, women. Special seating had been set aside in the rear balcony for mothers and small children.

Romar estimated that the service was an hour, but it didn't feel that way. The service had been in Tagalog, a language I was not fluent in. It consisted of singing, and then crying. I had been warned about the infamous crying from cousins on my father's side who were devout Catholics.

After the liturgical singing, a well-dressed preacher in a classy grey pinstripe suit, glasses, and slicked-back hair, stood at the pulpit crying. The entire congregation followed, crying, led by their preacher through a guilt and absolution session.

When the crying stopped, a very long sermon followed. I thought we were reaching closing prayers when the preacher began wailing again, and the congregation followed, crying again. What would Dominador have said about the long crying sessions? We didn't reach the end of the service until another session of singing was done.

Outside, I found myself surrounded by church members whom Romar lined up to meet me. "Would you like more information on our church? Maybe you'd like to visit one of our churches in America. We're everywhere." I had been known as the Orejudos relative who had traveled all the way from America.

Back in California, I asked my mother whether she knew her father was an Iglesian.

"That's what they told me growing up." Another secret I wasn't supposed to know.

"How did you stay Catholic?"

"Auntie Ising was Catholic and she raised me, so I became Catholic. My mother was also Catholic and I went to Catholic school all my life. I had been to an Iglesia service once when I was a little girl, but I don't remember it."

I told her about the crying. My mother had no response.

"Do you believe them about your father being Iglesian?"

My mother shrugged.

My father, who had been sitting on the sofa in the living room and overheard our conversation, exclaimed, "This is the first time I'm learning that my father-in-law was an Iglesian. I didn't know!"

My mother and I laughed.

She recalled how the nine children among Lolo and his siblings were divided: one daughter and four sons were Catholic, while the other two daughters and two sons were Iglesian. This had been my great-grandparents' compromise as Great-Lola Isabel was Catholic while Great-Lolo Alejo was Iglesian. There would've only been a handful of Iglesians in its founding days in contrast to its three million members today. There was a strong possibility that Great-Lolo Alejo might have personally known the man, Felix Manalo, who started the movement.

Lola Ising had been my mother's intimate connection to Catholicism on her father's side. The last time my mother saw Lola Ising alive, my mother found out she had converted to Iglesia ni Cristo.

"Why?" my mother asked, her voice shaking with anger as she reenacted her conversation with Lola Ising.

"Because everyone is Iglesian except me and I am lonely. No one comes to see me. They told me if I converted, I wouldn't be lonely and they could spend time with me because I could go with them to their church," Lola Ising replied.

It hurt my mother to know Lola Ising had converted, the strong Catholic matriarch who lived independently.

"Come to America. I can petition you to come and live with me and you won't be lonely," my mother begged.

"No, I'm old. I have bad knees. I can't travel."

And so, conversion became a matter of convenience to not be lonely, though I am not sure if the opposite of loneliness was even met. Great-Lola Isabel, who also converted to Iglesia a few years before her own death, probably out of the same reason that her eldest daughter did — to beat the loneliness — had told my mother, "Just because I converted doesn't mean I'm no longer Catholic."

As I planned my trip to the Philippines, I mentioned to my mother how I planned to visit Lola Ising's house. "There was a picture of me with a big bow on my head in her living room," my mother laughed as she placed her hand on the side of her head, feeling for the bow as if it were still there. "I was four. Maybe the picture is still there."

"Why didn't you grab that picture and Lolo's army picture in Lola Ising's living room when you went home for her funeral?"

"They're not mine."

"Lola Ising passed away. Whose was it going to be?"

"That's where they belonged."

It wouldn't have been the same for my mother to see the pictures here in America and not at Lola Ising's house. The pictures were forever her Auntie Ising's.

"Auntie Ising would call me her daughter. During the school year I was in Cubao, but every summer I went home to La Union, and that's what she told everyone, 'My daughter is coming to see me!'" My mother's voice was full of pride and giddiness. "I *was* her daughter." Lola Ising had adored my mother her entire life.

When Lola Ising died, only my mother and brother flew to the Philippines to attend her funeral. I was seventeen when I found my mother on the sofa. She had just received the news of Lola Ising's death. My father, home early from work, was sitting next to her, quiet. The scene didn't feel normal. She wasn't crying, and I couldn't tell if she had been, though I had never seen my mother so distraught.

My mother had a feeling about Lola Ising's death before she received the phone call from the Philippines. It had been morning and she was standing over the stove making breakfast when she felt a weight and breath against her neck, as if someone had been standing behind her, but no one was there.

Lola Ising—my mother's last intimate connection to her father by blood and storytelling—was gone.

During the last four weeks of my sabbatical, my boyfriend, Josh, joined me in the Philippines to backpack around the country. I took him to meet Lola Fely for the first and last time.

After being crammed with hundreds of people on a train, we still had to walk among hundreds on the street to get to Lola Fely's house in Cubao. My hands and feet had become swollen from walking in the heat while the humidity weighed heavy under Josh's eyes. It was easy to spot Josh. He was the only white person among a sea of Brown bodies.

The entire area where Lola Fely lived was now unrecognizable from the summer when I was ten. People lived on top of each other in makeshift homes made out of wood planks, pieces of concrete, and corrugated iron rooftops. The ceaseless noise of the metropolitan rail screeched directly overhead. The homeless slept on cardboards and lined the streets one after the other, while vendors sold fried bananas, balut, rosaries, and cigarettes.

"It wasn't always like this!" I yelled to Josh over the honking jeepneys, the sputtering tricycles, and car horns echoing up and down the street.

Lola Fely's house had been one of the oldest houses on the block to retain the traditional architecture from post-World War II, but now you couldn't even see it. She had the house built with the money she received from Lolo's military pension, putting the house in my mother's name as she was Lolo's sole heir, though she was an infant at the time. It was a house both Lolo and Lola would've shared together with the promise of filling it with many children.

When I was ten, an empty concrete lot was once at the front of the house. Children could ride their bikes, chase each other, and play dodge ball. I had been one of those kids. Now, there was no empty lot but makeshift homes for squatters, as well as the shoddy construction of a nightclub, pool hall, several sari-saris, and turo-turos.

My mother still remembered when two tamarind trees marked the location of Lola Fely's house. "Just turn left at the two tamarind trees," my mother had said. Lola Fely's house had been the lone house amidst rice paddies that stretched for miles. The only squatters were an elderly couple who had gained permission from Lola Fely to settle in the back lot. I could still hold onto images of Lola Fely's house when I was ten, but I couldn't imagine two tamarind trees and rice paddies everywhere.

My mother remembered little mounds of dirt near her home where the duende lived. When strange smells would emanate from those mounds, my mother was told that the duende were cooking their meals. Oh how they are being dishonored today. Lola Fely's beautiful house was ultimately torn down after her death. A cockroach-infested cheap hotel now houses a drug den directly atop the once duende homestead. A massive and wild concrete jungle hosts the dispossessed and displaced who have no opportunity to respectfully perform ancestral protocol, chanting "cayo cayo umadayo cayo," *give way give way so I don't step on you*, as there's not one hint of their existence to inform a passerby that the duende should be acknowledged. Electricity, light, and noise run all day long and have driven the duende out. It makes sense why they would leave. And it makes sense why they would curse those who no longer acknowledge them.

Lola Fely now lived with my uncle who had built his house next door, the space between the two homes the width of a single car driveway. My uncle decided to rent out Lola Fely's spacious old house. My uncle's house was a narrow two-story, two-bedroom home. He shared a bedroom with his wife and two teenage sons — one thirteen, the other eighteen. They all slept together in the same bed. Lola Fely shared a bed with her caregiver in the other bedroom.

This visit with my boyfriend was my last chance to see Lola Fely. This time, no stories could be told. No questions were asked. The only thing that mattered was sitting with her, holding her hand, playfully tracing the veins on her arms and her wrists, practicing my Ilocano, and hoping she would remember me.

All Lola Fely could speak now was Ilocano, her first language, a language she had once derided during my childhood when I showed any interest in learning it. Tagalog was the city language, the bourgeois language, the national language. Every other language seemed that of the poor, uneducated farmer.

She had spoken Tagalog and English fluently, but they would no longer come naturally to her. Senility had made the decision on which language she was allowed to speak. When my uncle encouraged her to speak English with me, she looked at her son shyly. I wasn't sure if she was pretending to not understand her son, or if she really didn't know.

"Come on, Lola, say something in English," I insisted, gently stroking my fingers up and down her soft arms.

She replied, "What did you say?" It was the only thing she said to me in English. Her words took me by surprise as she giggled.

"See! You remember how to speak English!" I said. "Speak English with Josh."

She batted her lashes at him with shy flirtatious eyes and then pursed her lips together and slapped my leg. Then she placed a firm hand on my thigh and held it there as I cuddled next to her on the sofa, and she laughed again, shy about speaking another English word.

When I was sixteen, Lola Fely told me to marry an Amerikano, which meant none other than a white man, believing we would have pretty mixed-race children. I had been sitting at my desk, quietly doing my homework under my fluorescent desk lamp, when from the dark corner of the room, she blurted out the suggestion while praying the rosary, reclined in her bed across from mine.

"Grammy! That's terrible!" I replied in disbelief, half-scolding, half-laughing.

She grinned, spiritual intoxication in her eyes, while quickly shooting her raised eyebrows at me as if swatting my response away as if it were a fly, and then went on murmuring the rosary, falling once again under a meditative trance.

Now that I was with Josh, was she satisfied? It didn't seem to matter. She was too shy to talk to him.

Lola Fely was still beautiful and elegant in her red floral duster and her soft dark hair, which my uncle made sure to color when her white roots would bloom from her scalp. She retained her smooth Oil of Olay skin and her dark brown hair which always made her look thirty years younger. I had never seen her with white or gray hair. She had always been diligent about having manicured nails, coloring her hair, and massaging Oil of Olay into her skin after washing her face every night.

At our last dinner together, Lola Fely could no longer feed herself. It was such a difference since I last visited her the previous month when she still could. Her twenty-year-old Visayan caregiver fed her now.

Right before she was put to bed, her eyes suddenly lit up in recognition and she did remember me and asked me when I was leaving for the states.

"Very soon," I told her.

Lola Fely became upset, threw a fit, and refused to be taken to bed even after her caregiver had already helped her up the stairs. She demanded to stay up and remain with me until I left.

When I tried saying goodbye, she rolled over on her bed, angry at me, as if it were a dirty trick that her granddaughter would come all the way from America for an evening to visit her and then leave so soon. I had visited Lola Fely a handful of times during my four-month stay in the Philippines, but she didn't remember me then. And now, on the last night when she finally remembered me, I was leaving her.

I tried kissing and putting my arms around her, but she refused to look at me. Her caregiver watched my attempts to coax Lola Fely into saying goodbye to me. As she lay on the bed, I massaged her legs like I used to do many years ago when I was eleven and we shared a room together. She jerked her body away from my touch.

Lola Fely's body was the last body Lolo had kissed and caressed and made love to. She had carried and birthed his only child.

"My life has been lonely," Lola Fely told me when I was seventeen. We had spent a lazy summer afternoon together before I moved away and started college. "When I meet up with the other army wives during reunions and ceremonies, I am the only one who lost her husband early. I see the others and how they had many years with their husband, having many children and many grandchildren."

"What is the one thing you always wanted in your life?" I asked, as if there were still time in her life to make her happy.

"To have many children," she replied.

From Lola Fely's small body on the bed, I looked at the framed 8x10 sepia photograph of Lolo on her dresser, a replica of the 11x14 photograph that had hung on Lola Ising's living room wall. I wanted the photograph, but I couldn't take it from her, even if she wouldn't have noticed it gone.

I stood in the doorway of her bedroom. She never told her husband, "Don't go." She knew she couldn't stop him from leaving. She couldn't stop me either. How much I wanted to stay but couldn't. How much Lolo wanted to stay but couldn't.

The last thing I saw of Lola was her back. I wondered what was the last thing Lolo saw of her.

Second Dung-aw

Before the bullet, you thought of your wife's delicate collarbones, the way you had kissed them tenderly on your last night together. You breathed in your daughter's heavenly scent from her little mouth to the few strands of hair that lined her bald, infant head. There were echoes of handshakes, kisses, and embraces from your eight brothers and sisters, and the strong arms of your parents wrapped around your neck as you had said goodbye.

These were your memories until you would no longer hurt, until your bones would wait to be exhumed from that sandy beach in Bacnotan.

Before the quiet would finally free you from the taste of metal in your mouth, an apparition of your wife—her smile, her smooth back, the stretch marks on her belly, her kisses on your neck—would appear until your eyes finally closed upon the horizon, the fine line marking the place between the last bit of light and the edge of darkness, between living and dying, between this last breath and the end. Your fallen body would lie upon a final bed of beach sand where you would drift beyond dreams, and for a moment, an apparition of your wife and daughter and all of your descendants would hoist you up before dying.

Determined to find Lolo's stone and bring it back to California, I traveled to La Union.

After breakfast at the hotel that my Uncle Franco managed and where my boyfriend and I stayed for our first night in my mother's province, I met Auntie Marina. Auntie Marina and Uncle Franco were my mother's first cousins. Amadeo was their father.

When Auntie Marina introduced herself, she shyly put her hand out to shake, not expecting to be greeted with the mano po as I gently took the back of her hand and pressed it to my forehead. She was surprised I still remembered.

I introduced her to Josh whom she shyly smiled at. Would she still have been shy if Josh had been Filipino?

Uncle Franco, also shy, told Auntie Marina the reason why I was visiting.

"Stone?" she asked.

"Stone," he said.

"Lolo's bato. Dakkel," I said, motioning with my hands the possible size of the stone I had never seen.

"I haven't seen it for a long time," she said.

"Do you know where it is?" I asked.

"It was at your Lola Ising's house last."

"I also want to visit Lolo's grave. Could we also visit Lola Ising's grave?"

"They are buried in different cemeteries and are far from each other," Uncle Franco said.

"I guess we can see Lola Ising's grave another time," I said, not wanting to trouble my aunt and uncle though deep in my gut I knew that I would never see Lola Ising's grave if I didn't see it now.

As we made our way to my mother's barangay by jeepney, I noticed how much La Union had changed with surf resorts crawling everywhere. I then realized why my mother hates coming home. "It's not the same," she said once.

As our route went from the paved streets of San Fernando to the bumpy back roads of Ubbog, we arrived at a stunning and still isolated landscape with tobacco fields and rolling hills.

"That's where your mother went to 1st Grade," Auntie Marina pointed to a small red bungalow. I imagined my mother—five-years-old, in flip-flops and a simple dress, skipping, surrounded by a lush landscape and blue skies everywhere.

My mother and I once told each other our dreams of home. I told her how I dream of Carson—our backyard, our house, our neighborhood. She told me how she dreams of Ubbog—her childhood barrio. I realized then the longing for home is different between us. We both reach for a home so stamped in our memory that it does not matter what forever homes we have made for ourselves today. I can still touch home whereas my mother can touch home only in her dreams. She knows Ubbog no matter how long she's been away. I can touch Ubbog through my mother who still dreams of living in the land of our ancestors.

I was hoping to now touch what my mother sees only in her dreams.

When we arrived at the site of Lola Ising's house, there was nothing left, not even a post, just the cement foundation, an old toilet with ivy growing out of it, scraps of clothes and shoes left behind by squatters, and a rectangular stone marker as if someone were buried underneath, bearing the inscription, "May 13, 1953." Uncle Franco and Auntie Marina didn't know what the date meant. Only when I returned from the Philippines did I learn from my mother that the date commemorated when they rebuilt the house after the War.

Lola Ising's house was the first home my mother had ever known. She was born within its walls when Japanese bombs dropped. There, she cried her first month's cries when her father had left his wife and child to fight as a guerilla in the jungles. And then when Lola Fely found herself a widow at the age of twenty-four, she had left my five-month-old mother to the care of Ising for the next five years. Lola Fely relocated to Manila to pursue a college education and establish herself as a teacher, which would give her the financial means to support her daughter.

My heart dropped to see the absence of the house. My heart dropped on behalf of my mother. My mother's dreams of home will remain dreams as her home never materialized into the walls I had hoped to touch on her behalf.

Uncle Franco and Auntie Marina claimed that Lola Ising's ghost could be seen traipsing the house at night. It was their family's reason for razing it. Despite Great-Lola Isabel and Great-Lolo Alejo's decision to split up their nine children between the Catholics and Iglesians — between the old religion and the new one — both sides still held onto their Indigenous spirituality with their undying belief in spirits and omens, which would always survive from the ancestors.

My mother hadn't known of her cousins' plans to raze it until I returned home with pictures of the ruins. Her reaction would be a mixture of surprise, rage, and grief. I wasn't naïve to ignore that Lola Ising's house held great value as one of the few surviving post-colonial homes in the area. The Narra posts and floorboards alone, Philippine mahogany, were valuable and rare. The house with its beautiful verandah and capiz sliding windows had survived American and Japanese bombs as well as the deliberate burning of colonial structures by Japanese soldiers. It had even been restored after the War as its 1953 marker attested, but it would not survive the fears, superstitions, and monetary interests of those descendants who razed it to the ground.

While I associated the house as Lola Ising's, my mother clarified how the house had actually belonged to her grandparents, Isabel and Alejo, who had built the house at the beginning of the 20th century to accommodate their growing family of nine children. It would be a century-old house. Two generations of Orejudoses had been born within its walls. My mother would be the last Orejudos born there.

Originally built in the traditional style, it had been constructed on stilts. The area beneath the house had been the bangsal, i.e., open-air storage space with a bamboo-trunk-laden floor where dishes were washed, where one went to use the bathroom and digos-digos (bathe), and where water jars were stored. After World War II, the bangsal eventually became the first floor with walls constructed on all four sides with a cement foundation. There would be a proper living room, kitchen, and dining room.

It only recently occurs to me that Isabel and Alejo's own parents *and* grandparents must have come through often to help cook, clean, and care for the nine babies. My siblings and I would be the sixth, and possibly last, Orejudos generation to walk within the ancestral Ubbog home before it was razed to the ground. Traces of ancestral skin cells had lined floorboards and walls, reaching out to great-great-great-grandchildren like ephemeral fingers wrapped around the discordant drumbeat of our pulse as we ran wildly around the house that summer in 1988 and left our own skin cells in the process, intermingling and becoming ancestral skin cells ourselves.

Over a century, the house would be built and rebuilt by Isabel, Alejo, and their three unmarried daughters—Ising, Cidad, and Ben. The house had lived through eras of American colonization, Japanese occupation, two World Wars, and stood long enough to witness the dawn of a new millennium.

Ultimately, *who* is left behind determines *what* we can hold onto.

To leave, to be diasporic, leaves us no choice but to relinquish any remaining vestiges of the past, and all the memories, history, and ghosts who linger there. There isn't any place for sentimentality when it comes to the fate of our ancestral homes.

An ocean away, my mother couldn't save her home. She had no say. None of us do.

The land would remain as if a century-old house were just a blip in the time quantum, not making any difference to the millennium of ancestors who had once before established themselves upon it.

Lola Ising's house, Ubbog, La Union
top: late 1950s; bottom: Lola Ising's funeral party, 1995

The last time my mother saw Lola Ising's house, 2006

The ruins of Lola Ising's house, 2009

Nothing remains but the cement foundation, an old toilet, and a marker commemorating when they rebuilt the house after World War II. Site of Lola Ising's house, Ubbog, La Union, 2009

Josh and I immediately went to work. We overturned rubble, dug our hands and arms in brush, and kicked up dirt. But the stone was nowhere.

Auntie Marina squatted, her hands in front of her as if feeling the shape of the stone that wasn't there. "It was right here," she said to herself, standing where the entrance of the house would've been. Auntie Marina didn't mention the mango or sarguelas trees.

Uncle Franco and Auntie Marina told me their brother, Ernesto, lived next door and probably would know where the stone might be.

She went to his house for help. Uncle Ernesto emerged from his home, a stone shack, with a cigarette in hand. He was wearing a tank top and shorts with holes and rips in them. His hair was sterling gray, while his eyes, his jawbone, his cheeks, and his build resembled a rugged twenty-year-old. Uncle Ernesto was four years my mother's junior and was far from twenty.

I greeted him with the mano po, feeling his gnarled hands, a farmer's hands, in my soft palm, the roughness of his knuckles pressed against my soft forehead.

"Manang Elsie's daughter," he said amused as he took a puff from his cigarette.

While Josh and I continued our attempts, Uncle Ernesto, Uncle Franco, and Auntie Marina watched us, chatting among themselves.

A dirt trail closed into a longer path ahead, covered in brush and bamboo. I yelled from across the ruins that Josh and I were going on a little hike up the path. They let us go without following.

The path should have led to a duende embankment and a little stream down below a bamboo bridge built by Lola Ising, a bamboo bridge I crossed two decades ago leading to a field where I bathed out in the open with a thousand dragonflies. I found neither bamboo bridge nor embankment but terraces of tobacco fields, bright green and gleaming under the sun. Lola Ising's tobacco fields, my mother's tobacco fields, which could've been mine, but now were Uncle Ernesto's.

"What do you want to do?" Josh asked as the terraces winked in the distance. I wondered if the open field I had bathed in two decades ago was a figment of my childhood imagination.

"I don't know." I really didn't. I didn't expect not to find it.

We made our way back to the ruins. Uncle Ernesto, Uncle Franco, and Auntie Marina stood around for one last look, their faces carrying blank stares.

"It was right here," Auntie Marina mimed its shape with her hands. Her brothers did the same, as if miming could will it into existence.

"When was the last time you saw it?" I asked.

None of them could remember. It could have been five years ago, ten years, yesterday, last night even. It hadn't moved. The stone had stayed in its usual little spot at the front corner of the house for years, untouched, unmoved, and everyone had gotten used to it, that for it to sit in its corner no longer meant anything. It had always been there, until one day it wasn't. It would disappear unnoticed, and the random day Dominador Orejudos' granddaughter would come all the way from America to retrieve it, she would never get to see it.

"Maybe someone took it?" Uncle Ernesto suggested.

"Why would anyone take it?" I asked.

"I don't know," he replied.

I then thought of the anthropologists, historians, museum collectors, and squatters. I also thought of Mother Nature naturally wasting it away.

We made our way next to Lolo's grave. I hoped to finally pay my respects. My visit back to the Philippines when I was ten was the only other time I would've had the chance to visit Lolo's grave. My mother had pointed out his cemetery as our car sped by, but we didn't stop. No one else seemed to think it important to pay our respects. Not even my mother.

The cemetery was a cramped place. There was no walking room between graves and each tomb either had a cement or marble marker raised two and a half feet above the ground. The groundskeeper, Uncle Franco, and Auntie Marina couldn't find Lolo's grave.

We jumped from marker to marker, standing on top of each tomb searching for him. They headed off in different directions. I stayed behind, only to get bitten by a red ant on the back of my hand below my thumb. A welt had formed. As I scrutinized the welt, I focused on where I was standing. It must be a sign.

Find me.

Where I was standing was covered by ivy and thorny brush, and with my bare hands, I tore away at the overgrowth. Underneath, I found him, a simple etched marble plaque, bearing the inscription:

R I P

Lt. Dominador C Orejudos

BORN JUNE 29, 1916
DIED MARCH 5, 1945

FAMILY REMEMBRANCE

When I called out to the others that I had found him, the groundskeeper hacked away at the remaining vines with his bolo to fully reveal Lolo's plaque. The plaque still appeared new as if he had been buried yesterday. An annual overgrowth of ivy would keep his plaque protected from the forces of heat and typhoon for decades.

Buried directly next to the left of Lolo's grave was that of a small child, bearing the inscription:

CESAr OrEJUDOS
BOrN FEb 22, 56
DiED MArH 16, 59

Unlike Lolo's plaque, Cesar's marker had been scrawled into a slab of wet concrete with a stick, then left to dry, leaving the penmanship and March misspelling of the anonymous scribe immortalized.

"This was our brother, Manang Elsie's favorite," Auntie Marina told me.

It suddenly occurred to me that this was the little adopted brother whom my mother referenced in passing nearly seven years ago. I had never known his name until now.

Cesar was the sixth of eight children. As was and remains the custom in the Philippines, a child from a large family in the barrio might be taken in by an aunt or uncle, particularly where a childless couple might adopt a favored niece or nephew. As Lola Fely was a young widow with my mother as her only child, baby Cesar had become a favorite to my mother from his infancy up until he was three-years-old, when she would visit Ubbog every summer during her childhood and adolescence.

Lola Fely had planned to adopt Cesar, in hopes of finally giving my mother a little brother. My mother had mentioned him only once when I had interned at an LA foster care organization. She had accompanied me to the Edmund D. Edelman Children's Courthouse for an adoption hearing. I had helped finalize the adoption of a six-year-old girl by her maternal aunt. It was Adoption Saturday. A hundred foster care children were finally being adopted after years in the system. As I was driving the 710 North on our way to the hearing that morning, my mother mentioned how at fourteen she had a little three-year-old brother whom she and her mother were in the process of adopting. Our drive to the courthouse must've triggered memories of the excitement she and her mother felt as they planned to make the long drive to pick Cesar up in Ubbog and bring him back to Cubao as her little brother. Sadly, he unexpectedly died of meningitis before he could be formally adopted.

I now stood before the bones of not only my mother's father but her brother.

Auntie Marina, Uncle Franco, and Josh left me to be alone. With my camera, I took several pictures of Lolo and Cesar's grave markers, zooming in, zooming out, cocking my camera at different angles.

In one life, they would've been father and son.

In another, they would've been uncle and nephew.

In this life, they eternally rest side by side—forever twenty-eight and forever three—while I at thirty-one surpassed them both in age. My Lolo and baby Uncle would never reach the status of Elder.

I imagine the magnitude of grief to lose a father whom one cannot remember and to lose a baby brother before his life has barely begun. My mother's life, my mother's mother's life, both stamped with grief that a stoicism was born to never show tears, even when on the verge of a dam breaking—the voice goes flat, the eyes become glass, and there's a silence so great that it is a wailing, a howling, if you stop to listen, to inhale it in.

I placed my hand on Lolo's plaque. What I desperately wanted to experience as sadness was simply the lost feeling of never getting to know a man I would never meet.

Auntie Marina's husband picked us up from the cemetery in his Forerunner. We sat crammed together on our way back to Auntie Marina's house for merienda and siesta.

"Do any of you know where Lolo was executed?" I asked.

"Near the beach," Uncle Franco replied.

"Do you know where?"

"Near here," he said quietly.

I didn't push further.

"It was such a long time ago," Josh whispered, as if his words provided an excuse, a respite, from this feeling of defeat. He was there to witness my search for Lolo's stone, but he could never understand. He might've thought his words brought comfort but it felt like a dismissal, that I should stop looking. That I should stop asking questions.

I would never stop.

As Auntie Marina cooked dinner, Josh watched *American Gangster* on their fancy cable television in the living room. They had one hundred channels but no flushing toilet.

I joined Auntie Marina in the kitchen and tried to make small talk. Auntie Marina was making Adobong Sitaw, a famous dish of my mother's, and I wondered if Auntie Marina and my mother had learned the recipe from the same person.

Auntie Marina and I sat at the dinner table together. Her Adobong Sitaw simmered on the stove. I felt like an anthropologist with my hands folded on the table, sitting up straight, my back not touching the back of the chair.

"I have not seen your mother for a long time. Not since Auntie Ising died. You should tell your mom to come home to the Philippines."

I didn't mention that my mother was in the Philippines less than six months ago. "I'll tell her to come and visit you."

"I'm sorry about our home. It's small. We are humble. Simple."

"Don't apologize. I wish we had stayed here last night than at that hotel. If we hadn't gotten into town so late, we would've wanted to stay here instead."

Auntie Marina smiled, her smile reminding me of my mother.

When Josh and I first arrived in La Union, Uncle Franco suggested we stay at the hotel. But I had told them that I wanted to stay with them. My response was not what they had expected as they told me how my other American cousins who visited had scoffed at their homes for lack of amenities and preferred to stay at a hotel where they could enjoy a hot shower, air conditioning, and a flushing toilet. I didn't think they would allow Josh and I to sleep in the same bedroom as we weren't married, but they had arranged that the best room in the house be ours for the night.

It was our last night in La Union, the province of my mother. My mother, who still believes in being a virgin until your wedding night and looks down on couples who live in sin. Josh and I had been dating for two years. My mother was not shy to make disparaging remarks about unmarried couples living together. And yet my mother, a war baby, was the daughter of her own antithesis. Her own parents could not marry until she was already six months inside her mother's belly. War had broken all rules of propriety. Churches and government buildings were bombed. Records—birth certificates, deeds — had been burned or lost. Priests went into hiding. Everyone went into hiding. If my grandparents had waited to consummate until they could be married, my mother would've never existed.

I think of my mother — a baby bridesmaid in utero.

I think of myself — the egg inside the baby bridesmaid, already there.

In the dark, I lay wide awake.

"I really thought we were going to find the stone. But you found your grandfather. You were meant to," Josh whispered, his face nestled against the back of my shoulder, our bodies two spoons.

My mind fluttered back to earlier in the evening when Josh and I decided to take a stroll through the streets of San Fernando. Before we hit the main road of Quezon Avenue, we made our way through a maze of the barangay's alleys, with people staring at us along the way, particularly at Josh whose fair skin attracted attention everywhere.

As we dodged potholes and broken sidewalks, we passed a few random businesses selling shoes, shirts, and perfume, and then took a detour, turning right. We found hundreds of pristine white stone steps leading up, up, up, somewhere. At the base of the staircase, a family of squatters had set up makeshift homes in the park. We had stumbled upon Heroes' Hill.

We climbed the long staircase lined with statues of Philippine national heroes and presidents. We occasionally stopped to look behind us, enjoying the spectacular sunset that blanketed all of La Union. When we reached the top, I could see how far the beaches stretched in La Union. I longed to feel sad but couldn't. I wanted to feel like a grieving granddaughter, but was it possible to grieve for someone you never knew? I didn't know anything about Dominador's childhood, what his favorite dish was, how his voice sounded when he sang, what songs he played on his violin. I wanted to know these things, feel these things as if I had lived them. I would always know things about him. But I would never *know* him.

I had always imagined he died by gunshot near a rice paddy, but his brother's grandson would tell me how he had been stabbed to death near the beach. My mother confirms the beach, but not the manner of how he died. "A gunshot," my mother confirms when asked point blank. From then on, whenever I would see old US army photos of other people's dads and grandpas from World War II and hear their stories of those who survived the Bataan Death March, I would wonder if they crossed paths with Lolo and shared a word, a laugh, a drink. A gunshot.

As I gazed from my left to my right, from south to north of the South China Sea, I knew my eyes brushed Lolo's execution site, as if all the beaches from Bacnotan to San Fernando belonged to him.

Dominador's name means "to want to be loved." How much I tried, so he might know how much he truly was.

Last Dung-aw

You visited your daughter in a dream once when she was a little girl. She could not look up to see your face — her head forced into a low bow before you. You told her, "You have forgotten me." She told you she had not, but she could not look up to see your face no matter how hard she tried to lift her head. She had woken up in a sweat, her heart racing, and in tears. When your daughter tells me these stories about you, she is still that little girl.

Questions still sit with me as I've spent seventeen years investigating how undeterred and invincible you must've felt after surviving the Bataan Death March. Your life had already been gambled on the most dehumanizing trail, and won. Even your infant daughter had survived the Japanese enemy unscathed with her enticing cuteness. Your rejoining the War as a guerilla was your last-ditch effort to ultimately winning the War. How angry and disillusioned you must've been to die at the hands of your own men. I retraced your Bataan Death March steps, stood before your bones, touched your tombstone, and held the hands and hugged the bodies and kissed the faces whom you held, hugged, and kissed, as if somehow I could touch you through the traces of ancient fingerprints and skin cells you might've shed and left behind.

I beg for your haunting, your apparition, but you never appear. Somewhere in tesseract time, you are still twenty-eight.

When I am forty-four and your daughter is seventy-seven, your daughter tells me she has traveled to places that first appear in her dreams. I too have traveled to places that first appear in mine. We are both surprised when new destinations feel familiar, not just familiar but we can recount these settings in old dreams as if they were old memories. Your daughter explains there is some trace of an ancestor whose memory is triggered through her body and she dreams of these old memories that do not belong to the current body she inhabits but rather to the DNA housed inside her bones.

Maybe your daughter and I both dream of your memories and all those family, friends, and detractors who told you theirs.

Maybe she eventually lives out moments of your life as they first appear in her dreams.

Maybe I eventually live out moments of your life as they first appear in mine.

And in this way, you are always alive.

STARRY KNEES

Star, the only girl among a sea of brothers and boy neighbors, would be the rough-and-tough little girl who'd unknowingly prove her competitive worth to her male counterparts by running around the neighborhood, shooting hoops, racing her bike down the street, aiming with her bow and arrow, and getting soaked in water gun fights.

One evening, I had been assigned to watch Star, seven, and her two little brothers, five and two. Their mother, my sister, would attend Easter Vigil Mass with their father. Father and eldest son were scheduled to be baptized into the Catholic Church that very evening and were already being prepped for the long ceremony ahead. It was to be a momentous occasion, but too long of a service, three hours to be exact, to demand the patience of small children whose attention-span was known to be very limited and whose irritability could explode into full-on meltdown when usual bedtime schedules were not strictly kept.

I was not a mother. It would be the first time I supervised three small children alone. My sister had managed five. I wondered if I could even manage one. Though Star could bear a three-hour late-night Church service, my sister decided it was best to leave Star behind to help me with the two younger boys. At seven, Star was already an expert on bedtime ritual—bath time, brushing and flossing teeth, changing into pajamas, and tucking in. She probably could've babysat them herself if we were back in colonial times.

It had been ten minutes before my sister was planning to leave when Star, playing tag with her two little brothers and the neighbor boy in front of their house, would take a rough tumble on the sidewalk after tripping over her flip-flops.

I didn't see her fall as a parked sedan across the street would block my view of the beautiful girl with dark, long, wavy hair hitting the pavement. I'd hear her laughing and screaming in delight when the sudden thud of her body against pavement would bring the joy to a halt and I'd see her body disappear behind the parked car. I wouldn't exactly know which body part hit the ground. I rushed across the street to find Star on her knees. The neighbor boy dropped down to his knees and asked if she was okay.

Earlier that day, Star and I amused ourselves in a silly game that involved my fingers as imaginary spiders tickling her flawless knees. She found the spiders delightful and had wanted me to tickle her knees over and over again while we watched movies on the sofa. Now, as I helped her to her feet, the first thing I saw was her tear-stained face staring at the pink flesh exposed on her knees which quickly gathered tiny red dots. Those red dots would flow very soon. I wanted to carry her into the house as she cried, but instead, I led her by the hand and together we walked home. Just then, I remembered my childhood of scraped knees. Star's own mother at ten-years-old had fallen off her bike doing daredevil stunts. She had scraped her elbows and ran home to our mother who didn't seem concerned how badly my sister had gotten hurt.

Most of the time, my sister and I—free-spirited, thrill-seeking daughters of the neighborhood—were too much for our mother to handle, so when we came home bruised, bleeding, and scraped, we tended to our wounds having learned the drill from the school nurse who handled our playground injuries with a rough hand. It's not that our mother didn't care. She just didn't soothe. One would think it came naturally with motherhood, but it doesn't necessarily happen that way. In my mother's time and culture, children were taught to suck it up. Children were seen as little adults, and still are in many parts of the world. Anything otherwise was regarded as unnecessary coddling. My sister learned to soothe from the absence of it.

The neighbor boy accompanied me and Star into the house. A ten-year-old gentleman. I sensed his concern and guilt as he sat on the living room floor with Star's eleven-month-old brother whom my sister had placed on the floor while tending to Star's wounds in the bathroom. My sister would respond differently to Star's injuries than our mother had done toward our own. She would personally tend to Star's wounds with extra care and comfort as Star screamed and screamed and screamed. I'd help by blowing on her knees while her mother applied antibiotic cream and bandages. The screams of the eleven-month-old and Star ping-ponged up and down the hallway between bathroom and living room, but the baby boy's desperate cries for his mother were no match to Star's piercing screams that demanded an end to human suffering.

Star screamed and screamed and screamed. I worried her screams would invite neighbors to call Child Protective Services. I wondered if I ever screamed like that as a child. There were tears, but otherwise, I had swallowed the searing pain, gritting my teeth in silence as the alcohol was applied to my open wounds.

I took strange delight and fascination in Star's scream, the kind of bloodcurdling scream that annihilated the air with machete blows, as if screaming, "Screw you!" to everything inside and outside of her.

If the whole world screamed like that, would people actually pause, listen, and stop attacking each other with their fists, guns, and knives?

Wounds cleaned and four bandages later, Star took her place on the sofa, hiccupping and continuing to wail her pain.

"Take deep breaths," her mother advised. "Together now." I joined them in taking deep breaths too to calm myself down.

My sister was running late for the momentous baptismal Mass, but she did not rush out the door. She continued to take long deep breaths with Star, and me, until Star finally calmed down and stopped wailing.

The neighbor boy continued to patiently wait on the living room floor, pretending to play with the baby, when he seemed to be waiting for, what he thought, a much-deserved scolding. After all, he had been the one who chased Star until she tripped over her flip-flops. He was a boy of ten, but the way he sat in the living room that evening listening to Star's piercing screams, he may as well have been a man awaiting his sentence.

"Kids fall. That's what they do," my sister calmly reassured Star. She would gently tell the neighbor boy to come back tomorrow for the Easter egg hunt and egg dyeing project in the afternoon. "Star will be fine and in tip-top shape tomorrow," she reassured him.

Star's mother slung the eleven-month-old to her chest and finally left for Mass.

"It's good you fell," I tell Star.
She looks at me like I am crazy.

"Your mom and I were always falling down and scraping our knees and elbows. I'm afraid children don't fall these days. We're living in a different time with cell phones and video games. Children don't seem to play outside anymore like you still do. I'm betting by the time you grow up, you won't meet a lot of people who had fallen as kids. It's good you fell."

She still looks at me like I am crazy. My words fail to provide comfort or any logic for that matter. Even I can't think of the right words sometimes.

She writhed in pain as she tried to snuggle next to me on the sofa. I had put on a movie, her favorite, *The Boxtrolls*, to distract her away from the pain. It doesn't work.

Star's two little brothers, snuggled next to me on my right, remained unphased and incognizant of their big sister's injuries as they were fully engrossed in the movie.

She writhed and writhed next to me until I couldn't take it anymore. I knelt down to her level, placed my hands on her shoulders, and looked her dead in the eye.

"What do you want me to do to stop the pain?" I asked. Her sad, teary eyes were beautiful. I wanted her to be okay again. I wanted her to smile and laugh and to never, ever be in pain ever again, but I know these wishes are impossible in life.

"I don't know," she said choked up in her tears. Of course she didn't know. She was seven. How could she know? I gathered her in my arms as she buried the whole of herself into my chest.

"Do you want me to kiss it?" I asked.

She nodded.

I bent down and slowly kissed the perfect skin above and below her knees. Her bandages continued to soak while I gave her long kisses, knowing somehow they were magical and sure. I looked up, and she finally smiled.

After the kisses, she requested the imaginary spiders to tickle her knees once more. She giggled as my fingertips lightly raced around the areas where her skin would grow stronger, carrying the battle scars of a childhood that her mother and I shared nearly thirty years before.

HAPPENSTANCE

I had no intention to go swimming my first morning on Olango Island when I spotted a young woman who was heading out in a bright yellow lifejacket with snorkel gear in hand. Before she descended the steps to the marine reserve, I told her that maybe I'd go in later. "You want to join me?" she asked. I wasn't planning to, but then she said, "It's better that we go together now as the tide might pull out in the afternoon."

It took me all of half a second to say, "Sure, do you mind waiting for me to change into my bikini and grab my gear?" She said she'd wait.

Her name was Willerie from Seattle. She was on a solo weekend island getaway while I had just arrived with my mother, aunt, and best friend to explore Cebu and the surrounding cities for the next few days. It was her last morning on Olango Island. She'd try to get some last-minute snorkeling in before she was to return to Cebu City.

The tide had pulled out so far that morning, but we were determined to walk as far out as we could to the deep. We had chatted about our Filipina-American lives while we walked about two hundred feet from shore with the water still barely above our waists. She was now living in Cebu with her Indian boyfriend, running a nonprofit together. They hoped to inspire young business leaders in the community. They had already been in Cebu for two months and were hoping they could make it to two years. She was skeptical that they would reach their two-year goal.

Despite her Filipino background, she expressed her concern that she wasn't Filipino enough in our Motherland. I could relate. We both were American-raised girls who weren't fluent in Tagalog and did not have parents who encouraged us to learn despite being daughters who held a love, longing, and fascination for our Motherland. I told her about my past reproductive rights activism in Quezon City and about the risks the work had entailed considering birth control remained largely inaccessible and abortion was still criminalized.

As we chatted away, we discovered that we had unknowingly worked in the same building in the Financial District in San Francisco. Me on the 27th Floor. She on the 15th. We marveled at meeting each other just now, theorizing that we were destined to meet in this tiny moment while snorkeling off Olango Island. I remembered the well-suited bodies in slacks, ties, dresses, and heels that crossed paths in the lobby every day. We were all there to do our 9 to 5, and that was it. That was our day. That was our life. That was the point of everything then.

We had laughed about our experiences on the public ferry just getting to Olango Island, when underneath the laughter had been a real fear as we each rode through monstrous waves in a boat that was barely a boat, completely ignorant and naïve of the fact that the equivalent of American safety standards was not necessarily paralleled in other countries.

When the water finally rose to our chests, we dove in, pummeled by the morning breakers. I was feeling nauseous when the appearance of teeming fish made it worth it to be battered by the waves.

Willerie had a bag tied around her waist with bread in it to feed the fish. She asked me if I'd like to feed them too. A part of me momentarily felt guilty as it was unnatural to feed them, but I couldn't resist the excitement of inviting the fish to us.

As we shredded the bread, the fish came like piranhas, not that I know what that feels like, but this seems to have come close. I watched as Willerie was besieged by strange and wondrous floating bursts of colors—of purple, green, blue, orange, red, pink, and yellow—all around her. I must have looked like I was exploding in underwater colors too.

The fish were eating from her fingertips. I was fascinated by her method and decided to do the same. It was the first time I felt small sharp teeth nibble at my fingertips, so I shredded the last of the bread and spread it all around. They began to swarm in a feeding frenzy. I noticed the sharp teeth from every little fish and became afraid that I would be eaten alive.

"Do you want more bread?" Willerie asked as I came up for air, overwhelmed by how many fish we had attracted.

"No, that's okay. One bit my finger. I'd rather not lose my fingers."

"Yeah, they'll do that. It tickles."

I didn't think it tickled. It terrified.

We swam for a good while longer when I opted to chase the fish rather than them chase me for food. It's hard to say how long we had been out there. The simple act of swimming with the fish could've taken twenty minutes or forty. Every second seemed swallowed as we focused on the fish that swarmed all around in colorful explosions. There was a magic about the ocean and the intimacy that water can bring when you're in it with someone else, drawing a fear and longing, maybe because to be completely submerged subconsciously reminds us of that original haven of floating in our mother's watery womb. Willerie felt like a birth twin. We could've been in that water forever, until tired arms and tired legs reminded us of our mortality, forcing us back to shore. It was Willerie who proposed to head back.

By the time we climbed the stairs from the marine reserve back to the resort, Willerie was informed by our resort hostess that the next private ferry was leaving in twenty minutes as a typhoon was approaching and this would be her last chance to get back to Cebu City before it hit. All public boats would then be detained until the typhoon passed, which could take another day or two. The Coast Guard would not be letting any boats cross after this. She rushed back to her room and packed. Willerie's weekend was over while mine had just begun on Olango Island.

As she hurriedly packed, we exchanged Facebook profiles, phone numbers, emails, and hugs. We had at most one hour together that morning, when you impatiently pull out the most important parts of yourself to share. We agreed that there could have been no better time to meet than when we had. Not at the Financial District where we went to and fro as drones, but we had to meet on this lonely island, two gals snorkeling among a myriad of fish, sharing the expanse of the sea.

HOW NOT TO DROWN

I.

I didn't learn to swim until I was sixteen. I grew up twenty minutes from the ocean, but it doesn't mean you know.

The blood of island people runs through my veins. Still, it doesn't mean you know.

Women in my family had grown up by the ocean. Still, they didn't know.

Why not? you ask.

Women couldn't.

Just as they couldn't ride bikes as my mother told me, *My Lola said girls who rode bikes broke their hymens, and if your hymen was broken, a man would never want you.*

Maybe the ocean was seen as sensual. The same exhilaration felt during orgasm. Again, another belief orgasms were not meant for women.

Swim. Now. I command myself as I snorkel in Fiji-Sangat-Leyte-Maui-Oahu-Kauai-Menjangan-Vieques.

Don't hyperventilate. Don't question the physics.

And yet the questions still flood—*How is it possible to stay afloat?*

Brightly colored fish swim past my fingers, temporarily reminding me what I have always known in the womb.

After a day of work in San Francisco while waiting for the bus, I'd imagine swimming to the tops of skyscrapers, when I would suddenly think of drowning—the waters closing in like an infestation of ants.

I remind myself, *You know how.*

II.

I learned to swim at sixteen, which may be considered not that late, but I was old enough that the fear of water seeped deep into my psyche than if I were to have learned at seven or eight when everyone else had learned. I learned to ride a bike at twelve when everyone else had learned at five. With learning to bike, I was not so afraid. With swimming, I can never shake the fear of drowning that greets me when I first step into water, and it takes rational reminding that swimming is an act of physics—*I will not drown if I just swim as I have learned all of those decades ago.*

My mother could only dream of swimming.

My mother eventually learned to swim at forty-nine. Fear, still there. For both of us.

Throughout college and law school, which amounted to seven years total, I swam at least three to four times a week to every weekend to almost every night at one point, swimming the freestyle for two straight hours without pause—to shake the fear of water, to build my stamina in it. In the deep end with each stroke, I'd stare at the pool floor ten feet below as if I were flying. Even the lifeguard would take notice and marvel at my endurance when I'd finally climb out of the pool and submerge myself in the jacuzzi, my muscles melting in the heat and steam, transforming from frightened human to peaceful jellyfish.

You are such a good swimmer with good form, but what does praise matter when the fear of drowning dictates first?

III.

At forty-four while visiting a Pinay sister in The Bahamas, she would simply tell me to speak with the ancestors while we swam. This ancestral communication should have come as second nature to me. Instead, she switched the light on in my brain. My Pinay sister could not ride a bike, but she could swim in open water for miles.

There's a sadness here amidst the beauty. Do you feel it?

The blood of island ancestors ran through both our veins. My Pinay sister, having grown up a Diasporic child in The Bahamas, told me of the Lukku-Cairi's absence, a resounding mourning echo between land and sea. She reminded me that the turquoise waters were never just paradise but a final resting place, where slave ships had discarded three million Africans into this very sea. Our own Filipino ancestors circumnavigated the world as slaves on Spanish galleon ships. And now, four hundred and thirty-five years later, we Diasporic granddaughters were swimming in their space.

Please, ancestors, she implored as she swam half a mile out to explore a rock in the middle of the sea.

Please, ancestors, I implored when the age-old fear suddenly cut me loose.

The next morning while snorkeling, I spent a peaceful minute treading by myself, not caring at all about the fish, but I calmly watched the swaying surface of the water as I felt, for once, a gentle immersion that accepted me wholly in return.

LAST THREE DAYS IN TWENTYNINE PALMS

I acknowledge the Maara'yam (Serrano), ʔívíȋuqaletem (Cahuilla), Nüwüwü (Chemehuevi), and Pipa Aha Macav (Mojave) as the Traditional Custodians of Mar-rah, and pay my respects to their Elders past, present, and emerging, and that the land be restored to the Indigenous nation or nations that previously had sovereignty over the land. I extend that respect to all Indigenous peoples today. I recognize this land acknowledgment is limited and engagement is an ongoing process of learning and accountability.

My sister was leaving Twentynine Palms. As much as I was used to the fact that my sister and her family moved quite often due to my brother-in-law's career aspirations, this move made me particularly sad as I had come to affiliate Twentynine Palms and Joshua Tree with my sister. It would no longer be the case.

My sister's final departure from Twentynine Palms to the East Coast would be July 30th. As I live in the San Francisco Bay Area, I had driven first to Carson, my hometown in LA for my parents' 51st wedding anniversary. COVID hit last year and we were not allowed to celebrate their big 50th. We were all making up for lost time since receiving our vaccinations.

I would be in LA until the first week of June. I didn't know when I'd see my sister again.

I decided to spend three days in Twentynine Palms to see my sister and her five children for the last time. Her husband had already relocated and started a new job. My sister had been left with the task of packing up the house and the kids before joining him.

My brother's twelve-year-old daughter, Casey, accompanied me on this last trip from LA to Twentynine Palms to spend time with my sister's thirteen-year-old daughter, Star. The girl cousins remain close, especially as my sister's daughter is the only girl among four boys.

Before we left my brother's house, I told Casey to pack her hiking gear as my sister lived a few miles from the north entrance to Joshua Tree National Park.

By 2 PM from the 10 East, I missed the 62 East exit towards Twentynine Palms and had to turn around at the next exit. Fortunately, a bathroom break was needed. I parked at one of several gas stations off Indian Canyon Drive and nudged Casey awake. I told her I needed to use the bathroom. The temperature gauge in my car read "103." Casey, still groggy from her nap, said she didn't mind waiting in the car, but I might as well be committing murder if I left her in the car for even five minutes.

"It's air conditioned in the store. Your dad will kill me if I leave you in the car."

Casey reluctantly got out of the car, and as expected, we were greeted with a blast of heat that felt like an inferno. I told my niece to use the bathroom even if she didn't feel like she needed to. I bought her whatever snacks she might like, though my sister-in-law had already packed her a goodie bag. Casey at first declined saying she already had snacks. I told her you could never have too many, especially as we had another hour or two to get to my sister's house.

Finally on the 62, Casey did not fall asleep again but observed the expansiveness of the landscape. When one drives out of LA into the High Desert, one can feel and see the dividing line as the city disappears and Joshua Trees spring like arms reaching out from the cracked earth. Extraordinary rock formations line up along the highway, signaling a vast kingdom. We talked about the existence of God, colonization, and racism. Casey had questions, all spurred by the High Desert which surrounded us: Who lived here, then and now?

By the time we arrived at my sister's house at 3:30 PM, the temperature gauge on my dashboard read "105." We hurriedly unpacked the car and were saved by the air-conditioning of my sister's house. I double-checked that we unpacked everything as I could only imagine things literally cooking if left behind.

As we stepped out of the car and onto the curb where a strip of grass or lined path of rocks should've been, there were three little mounds of dry sandy dirt signaling ant colonies underfoot. I told Casey to be careful not to step on them. My mother would've thought these mounds were evidence of duende homesteads, and without consciously thinking about it, I carefully took steps not to disturb them while unpacking the car—pleased and delighted that Twentynine Palms had not driven the duende out.

As soon as we walked in through the door, my sister reported how her van wouldn't start and that I had to bring her to the mechanic as well as pick up food for dinner. While it was not exactly the greeting anyone expects after a three-and-a-half-hour drive through the egregious traffic of LA and the Inland Empire, I was ready for mishaps like this. She had just installed a new battery and guessed it was an electrical problem. I thought of the 100-degree-plus heat their van sat in every day in the driveway. It wasn't far-fetched to think something had eventually melted and finally broke over the six years they had been living there.

My sister's house had become a melee of boxes and piles of books and art and school projects and clothes and other towering things. What was I looking at exactly?

I hadn't sat down for ten minutes when my sister said the tow truck was arriving soon and I would have to drive her to the mechanic. We left all six children behind, the eldest fourteen and the youngest seven. My sister trusted they would be fine without us for an hour.

The mechanic's diagnosis was that the van would not be ready for the next two or three days. My visit came just in time.

We picked up tacos for dinner and then holed ourselves up with the A/C set at a comfortable 75 degrees until the sun finally set.

All that separated my sister's yard from the expansive desert was a black, metal grill fence. Besides her neighbors to her left and right, she had none beyond the backyard. It was nothing but desert and thousands upon thousands of shrubs for miles and miles that stretched to the mountains in the horizon.

By early evening, the temperature had cooled to a comfortable 99. In the twilight, my sister, nieces, nephews, and I played jump rope and Double Dutch in our flip-flops under pink cotton candy clouds that streaked across the sky like outstretched eagle wings.

Behind my sister's yard under pink cotton candy clouds streaked across the
sky like outstretched eagle wings
Twentynine Palms, 2021

Before my sister and I settled down and slept in her bed, I asked if we should go hiking tomorrow. I was hoping to hike the unmarked trail to the Heart Rock as we had done a couple of times before—the first to commemorate her winter birthday, the second to commemorate my fall birthday which coincided with the publication of my first book.

"Unless you want to hike at 5 AM," she sighed.

We would not be hiking at 5 AM. We would not be hiking at all. The temperature reached a searing 108 every day we were there.

"We're indoor people for most of summer."

The next morning, Casey accompanied my sister's four children to the corner store a quarter-of-a-mile away to pick up snacks. The nine-year-old who was prone to asthma attacks, and particularly as we were still living in the time of COVID where he faced the highest risk, stayed behind.

We spent the morning quietly milling over our phones when news broke regarding the recent discovery of a mass grave of 215 children in Tk'emlúps (Kamloops). Her son had overheard us talking about the 215 children, and proceeded to ask us questions—whether the children were his age and why were they taken away from their homes and why would the Canadian government erase the cultural identity of these children by sending them away to these schools in the first place and then covering up who they were in these unidentified mass graves.

We gave him answers. They weren't easy but we didn't lie. We didn't sugarcoat the fact that the US and Canadian governments were both equally guilty of eradicating Indigenous culture and their peoples through systemic genocide. It seemed a compelling moment right then and there as many Americans seemed to hold onto an idealized view of Canada—of being the polite country, the nice country, with gun control laws and a non-racist society, when the country's past and continued treatment toward its Indigenous communities was not any better than the United States. White supremacy and genocide know no bounds.

When I was nine, the same age as my nephew, a Native ceremony at my own Catholic elementary school was held on school grounds, an area where we ordinarily held morning exercises for the Pledge of Allegiance. It was October 1986.

My nine-year-old self cannot remember the name of their people, but one of the school administrators at the Office of Religious Education was of Native descent. Her father, a very elderly man, led the ceremony and was elaborately dressed in their nation's regalia. He appeared frail with lines etched across his tan face, while his beaded feather headdress adorned his head as if he were an old king. He had summoned a blessing in their Native language, holding a bowl of burning sage as they ceremoniously walked from one end of the lot to the other. The entire school, approximately two hundred and forty students, watched in awed silence.

His grandson, Chris, a young man in his twenties, who had been volunteering as a teacher's aide under his mother, was dressed in nothing but a breechcloth. His shoulder-length brown hair had been tied into a ponytail while his head was adorned in a simple headdress of feathers, not as large or ornate as his grandfather's. His elbows and ankles were adorned with a simple string of feathers. He had on light-brown fringe moccasins. His eyes that usually twinkled behind steel-rimmed glasses were now somber without them while his grandfather led the prayer. I had worried whether

Chris was cold as the morning air was chilly and the skies were cloudy, his bare skin fully exposed to the elements. Chris slowly led the procession while his grandparents followed closely behind. The ceremony was held the week of Columbus Day. They never held the ceremony again at my school and I never would witness another Native ceremony during my childhood.

Chris in his regalia made me see him differently, that he carried something generations old. He wasn't just a teacher's aide in that moment. He had become a warrior before my eyes.

After the ceremony, we resumed our 4th Grade classroom instruction. My teacher, a German Carmelite nun, rather than discuss the symbols of the ceremony and their regalia—the feathers, headdresses, the prayer, the burning sage, and the procession—had instead commented how "Native Americans no longer exist." She wanted us to believe that what we had just witnessed was simply a performance and not an authentic ever-present Indigenous meaningful spiritual ceremony.

My fellow classmates and I, a classroom predominantly made up of Filipino and Mexican children, were learning Indigenous erasure from our white Catholic schoolteacher despite what Chris and his family intimately shared with the entire school that very morning: that Native peoples are *still* here and have not been erased. While she lauded the retention of her own pure German identity, she denied the existence of Native peoples, believing their bloodlines were erased by colonization and blood quantum. In 1986, "settler colonialism" was not yet coined a term. However, as my teacher was a Carmelite nun who studied the history of Catholicism and its proselytization, she would've been aware of the removal of Indian children from their homes and their placement into residential schools, the "breeding out" of Native peoples through the rape of Native women and girls, the coerced commingling with white European settler blood, and ultimately the systemic genocide of Native peoples to warrant her belief that "Native Americans no longer exist." If she felt her 4th Graders had the capacity to understand her lessons on abortion, she would've given herself reason to believe that we could equally handle learning about what had happened to Native peoples. But she never mentioned it.

Thirty-five years later, I would wonder whether Chris' near nakedness in his Native regalia had made my 4th Grade teacher shudder as she stood in her long, black veil and floor-length, brown tunic, completely covered from head-to-toe, not one inch of skin showing except the center of her face and her pale slender hands. Our Carmelite teacher's evasiveness regarding any discussion following the ceremony seemed to reflect the Church's age-old stance toward Native peoples — that they provoked lasciviousness and impropriety in showing skin so boldly, thus concluding the Church's reasoning that Indigenous peoples must be "uncivilized" and "needed saving."

The children of Tk'emlúps felt that much closer.

By the time the rest of my nieces and nephews returned from their morning walk, we did not talk about the 215 children again, though maybe the nine-year-old privately discussed what he learned that morning with his siblings and cousin.

Casey had been on her period and was exhausted and dehydrated with a migraine. The morning had already climbed to 91 degrees by 9 AM. The simple quarter-of-a-mile walk from home had unexpectedly become the longest walk of her life. After feeding everyone a hearty breakfast of sweet and savory pastries that my sister and I had picked up from the bakery, we sent Casey off to bed with some Advil. She spent half the afternoon napping in the master bedroom while we'd gently nudge her awake to drink water every so often.

The rest of the afternoon, I helped my sister run errands while all the kids, except the youngest, stayed behind playing board games, drawing, watching cartoons, or playing video games. My sister needed to pick up her son's asthma prescription and groceries for the week. My youngest nephew was eager to help with errands, especially grocery shop, picking out the best fruit or vegetable, even if it meant stepping into 108-degree heat while jumping from car-store-car-store-car and chasing air-conditioned places.

At home, Star made everyone sandwiches of grilled chicken, bell pepper, and cheese on a hoagie roll with fries for lunch, while my eldest nephew prepared dinner of roast beef with green beans.

In the evening, my sister had put on *Into the Woods*—the 1991 filmed live musical, not the 2014 Disney movie version. It had been our favorite growing up and so the kids, my sister, and I all laughed and danced and sang to the songs in the living room.

As the kids were finally settling down for bed, I snuck outside to the backyard. I should've been concerned about snakes or spiders as I was in my flip-flops, shorts, and a tank top, but I wasn't. It was shortly before 10 PM, 95 degrees with a little wind. I stared up at the sky. Tonight would be the last time to properly admire the stars, when my sister was still here. Though there was a little haze, the stars still shined brightly.

I had made it a point to know the names of the Indigenous communities of the land—Serrano, Cahuilla, Chemehuevi, and Mojave. Streets not far from my sister's house had hinted at their existence as the streets had been named after them. At the time, I was not aware that each community had an Indigenous name that they preferred to be called versus the colonized names that they were given by Spanish missionaries and settlers.

Though modern development remained largely absent from the desert to preserve the brilliance of Joshua Tree National Park, there was still the overwhelming absence of the Indigenous communities that had once lived on this land, back when there were no borders. There is the federally recognized Twentynine Palms Band of Mission Indians, descendants of the Chemehuevi, and we were on their land, a land once teeming with not just the Chemehuevi, but with tens of thousands of the Serrano, Cahuilla, and Mojave, long before white men came, stole their land, changed the names of their peoples, endangered their languages, endangered their dances, endangered their customs, and removed their children from their homes by orders of the federal government.

As my family are immigrants to LA, the Indigenous name of my hometown in Carson is Suangna, whose name in Tongva means "place of the rushes." Suangna's population had thrived for thousands of years up until the 1850s, when by the end of the 19th century, their existence and lives had been completely uprooted like the rest of the Native population in California through Spanish land grants and industrialization. I thought of the lush backyard of my parents' house. My grandparents and parents had created an expansive burgeoning garden filled with hundreds of varieties of succulents, cacti, and flowers, as well as a vegetable and fruit tree garden endemic to their Ilocos motherland. It seemed my grandparents and parents were trying to replicate the lush landscape of their Motherland but were ultimately led to cultivating the rich soil of Suangna land.

It seems magical coincidence that my parents would ultimately migrate to a city whose own Indigenous name means "place of the rushes." Rushes are aquatic grass-like plants that thrive in boggy soils under fluctuating water conditions, much as my father's hometown, Lapog, named after a native Ilocano grass, means "land dependent on rain."

It seems the ancestors across lands wholly understood the inescapable necessity for water and thus named their lands as a constant reminder for this invaluable life-sustaining force in case we ever forgot. Many cities of the colonized world are now named after white men, when the land had a name given by Indigenous ancestors to inform us that no one owned it, but that we belonged to it, that we had an ever-present fiduciary duty to act in the land's best interest to ensure our own survival.

Now in Twentynine Palms, I'd learn the Indigenous name is Mar-rah, which in Maarrênga'twich (the Serrano language) means "place of little springs and much grass." The area was abundant in food, medicinal plants, and other countless resources through the Indigenous communities who had utilized their farming skills and cultivated a large garden from the water they irrigated from the Oasis. That all changed in 1855, when a white surveyor changed the name of the Oasis to "Twentynine Palms." It had marked the beginning of the end of an Indigenous way of life. Their land was taken by the state and sold to a private company without their permission or knowledge.

My sister and I are daughters of a land also of little springs and much grass. My sister and I are the daughters of men and women who came from Ubbog and Lapog. Ubbog is derived from the Ilocano word meaning "little springs," while Lapog is derived from LapoLapo, a native Ilocano grass to pasture animals.

According to our mother as she recollects her childhood, countless little springs bubbled up from the earth in Ubbog during the rainy season. Now, there are none. According to our father, the grass of Lapog also springs up during the rainy season and fortunately still exists.

Lapog is more specifically derived from the local term, "Lap-Lapog," which means "rain-fed land" or "land dependent on rain." Lapog, like Mar-rah, like Suangna, had its Native name replaced by a colonized one. Lapog became San Juan in 1961. Our father was seventeen when they changed the name of his beloved town. "Lap-Lapog" does not simply mean unirrigated land. Our father explains how the term "Lap-Lapog" holds a multi-layered Indigenous understanding of not just the grass as rain-fed, but that *all* living things on that grassland are rain-fed. When there is no rain due to a climate crisis, all living things face a crisis of survival where a curtailment of the excess of human activity must be heeded immediately. The erasure of the Native name reflects the erasure of the environmental custodial understanding behind that name on how precolonial communities had cared for their land for thousands of years as they strove to prevent the degradation and depletion of their land's natural resources.

The Native name never holds a simple scientifically short meaning. Instead, it holds a complex understanding of the symbiotic relationship between living things and the land they inhabit.

For Ubbog and Lapog, their Ilocano names suggest what the inhabitants would've expected of the land's agricultural and environmental yield during and after the wet season. Their names would've also signaled the time of year when the wet season *should* occur.

Our mother explains how the springs of Ubbog no longer exist as twenty years after her birth, the earth had cracked open and created gullies. The land was shifting and changing, just as the ecological landscape of Mar-rah itself had shifted and dramatically changed in half a century due to white settlers who invaded their land, began mining operations, and brought their cattle, which depleted the water and land resources once tendered and cultivated by the Indigenous communities of Mar-rah.

For our father and his townmates, it is always Lapog. For Native descendants who remember and pass down the origin stories of present-day Twentynine Palms, it is always Mar-rah.

As I stared up at the hazy but brilliant stars in my sister's backyard, the desert lay boundless and immense in the darkness. I thought of the children in Tk'emlúps, but I also thought of the Indigenous children of this High Desert, the bones I might've been standing on where a housing development for US military families now stood, and my sister's family had been one of them.

Out loud, I acknowledged the Serrano, Cahuilla, Chemehuevi, and Mojave of the land I now stood on. Out loud, I honored the children in Tk'emlúps, and who they had been. Out loud, I acknowledged the survival, resilience, and resistance of all Indigenous peoples of this continent.

The week before, I had a very public online confrontation with a white man from Canada who continues to run a Filipino history and folklore website specifically aimed at a Filipino audience. He had operated online for years largely under an audience's assumption and belief that he was Filipino. When his whiteness had been exposed, he placed the onus on his online audience that they should've known better about his white identity, as if absolving himself of his failure to disclose his whiteness in private misleading emails with online members who believed he was Filipino. He went on to further claim his respect for the Filipino community through his marriage to a Filipino woman, as if that were sufficient in lieu of actual in-person involvement with our community. Not one among his expansive followers could produce one picture of him meaningfully participating and engaging with our community at an in-person event despite his self-proclaimed involvement with our community for years. While still under the ambiguous guise of a Filipino man, he had claimed himself an authority on precolonial Philippine history and mythology. His use of problematic language had been deeply insensitive regarding revered ancestral deities and supernatural beings. He had also undermined the value of our Oral Tradition by prioritizing written documentation by white male historians while discrediting our culture's ongoing shamanic practices of our Babaylanes, who not only exist historically but currently practice as Indigenous modern-day healers in the Philippines and the Diaspora. When his white identity had been exposed, a Pinay community member had publicly shared email correspondence with him dated two years prior, where he dissuaded her from exploring our current Babaylan practices when she inquired his opinion. From the context of their correspondence, she assumed he was Filipino as she interchanged between Tagalog and English. He responded as if he were a legitimate Filipino authority without ever clarifying his whiteness. Disengagement from him was the best decision though the public confrontation left many online community members to take sides. Those in support of him argued, "At least someone is doing it" as if he were a reliable authority to feed us our culture through his own racialized interpretation, as if there were no fetishization behind him doing so, as if our own community were incapable of passing down our own knowledge and history, as if we hadn't already tried. I received threats of violence for calling him out when his white identity had finally been exposed. After finding myself a target of such threats, it had been my mother who helped me make sense of the deeply ingrained sentiments that encased me and our community, imparting her own sarsarita on the matter: (1) Wala kang utang na loob, as if we owed this white man our gratitude; but more significantly, (2) dacami ti gungguna dagiti napateg nga puraw.

Despite the detractors, I also received several messages of support from the Filipino community, but it was the timely comforting words from outside the community, from a highly esteemed Diné writer who also lived in the High Desert and witnessed what had happened and offered her own reassuring support and solidarity, "These imposters land hard on hundreds of years of colonization trauma within POC like us. It's such a violation and a type of soul-theft. But we are made of strong stuff—our ancestors' resilience in our blood."

As I acknowledged out loud the Indigenous communities of Twentynine Palms in that moment, I realized my very own personal brush with white supremacy, even if it was just a cyber face.

Three shooting stars then appeared—one from the South, and then another from the East, and then the last from the North.

When I slipped back into the house through the rear door, my sister did not ask where I had gone. She was getting her children ready for bed, setting a timer for the two youngest boys brushing their teeth. "Two minutes! Go!" she yelled from the living room.

I chose not to divulge many details with my sister about the confrontation with the white man in Canada. She was in the middle of packing up her life and moving across the country.

That last night in Twentynine Palms, Casey and Star slept in the same bed in Star's room, while my sister and I slept in the same bed in the master bedroom. We slept side by side like our grandmothers had done long ago, when their sisters had visited, not just from out of town but from out of country. Lola Fely and her sister Gunding. Lilang Atang and her sister Poten. We little girls would eavesdrop on their low thrummed conversations in Ilocano as they lay side by side in the dark, both their voices an almost twin range, these Lolas, nearly forgotten shamans, conjuring our maternal ancestral homes in the Ilocos—Uyaoy and Labnig—reminiscing of their girlhoods when granddaughters and great-granddaughters hadn't even yet been a dream.

Both our grandmothers had been second to the youngest daughters who both had been close to their baby sisters. I was second to the youngest while my sister was the youngest. Star was second to the youngest granddaughter while Casey was the youngest granddaughter. We sisters — daughters, granddaughters, and great-granddaughters — loved each other in these birth-ordered pairs. It was an authentically coincidental pairing that spanned generations.

During her years at Twentynine Palms, my sister had the beloved flowers of our grandmothers tattooed on her left arm. An orange carabasa flower for Lilang Atang, our paternal grandmother. A red cayanga (gumamela) for Lola Fely, our maternal grandmother. Other tattoos on her body included sampaguita blossoms, paying homage to the national flower of our seven-thousand-island archipelago, as well as the delicate flight of dandelion seeds representing her five children. Her body had become a walking garden of our Motherland, ancestors, and descendants.

On the last morning before returning to LA with Casey, I had driven my sister to work. She was a bookkeeper and administrative manager at a Catholic Church. She had given us a tour of the grounds — the old non-operable convent that was now her office, and the old non-operable Catholic school with its classrooms and neglected playground. I thought again of the children at Tk'emlúps, once the largest residential school in Canada, operated by the Catholic Church. The irony of standing once again on grounds considered holy yet possibly holding secrets whispered deep underground, waiting to be heard.

In her last years in Twentynine Palms, my sister had encountered anti-maskers, Proud Boys sightings, and parishioners in her own Church who did not believe in the severity of COVID and spewed anti-immigrant sentiment, yet made an exception for my sister as they viewed her as having come from the "proper" immigrant family when there has never been such a thing. It would be naïve to think the spectacular beauty of the desert overruled the vitriol that pumped into this human landscape. At the same time, the desert's hypnotic beauty could keep tourists and current residents alike ignorant of Indigenous dispossession, displacement, genocide, and environmental atrocities committed on this land before.

In spite of all that, my sister was able to raise her children idyllically. She and her family hiked, camped, rock climbed, attended community events, supported local artists, and made very dear and trustworthy friends.

And now my sister was leaving.

How opportune this moment of facing off a cyber white supremacist in Canada the week before, how a Diné writer from the High Desert reached out with comforting words in the aftermath of that face off, my sister's van breaking down just when I arrived, the recent discovery of Indigenous children's bodies in Tk'emlúps, my late night acknowledgment of the Indigenous communities in my sister's backyard and the three shooting stars that consequently followed, the coincidences of where we live and where we find ourselves no matter how short of a time, in the land of "little springs and much grass" wherever we are in the Diaspora, in Ubbog, in Lapog, in Suangna, in Mar-rah, in another's land that was stolen by settlers of the same white skin who stole our archipelago for four hundred and twenty-five years, who stole the continent we now live on, and the legacy and ignorance of it still ongoing, how everything changes, how everything connects, and even the High Desert that appears virginal is far from virginal and had undergone great change and bloodshed and reorganization that we could only imagine. What seemed a mish-mosh intersection of events had culminated into a meaningful convergence in the High Desert in those last three days, where magic, ancestral magic, was still peeking through to fill the impending absence in my own microcosm—my sister ultimately leaving with her five children.

I asked my niece to snap a picture of me and my sister one last time. Palm trees and the mountainous backdrop of Joshua Tree National Park swept behind us far in the distance as we posed together, holding each other close.

THE BEGINNING OF LEAVING

I acknowledge the Ngarluma, Mardudhunera, Yaburara, Yindjibarndi, and Wong-Goo-Tt-Oo as the Traditional Custodians of Murujuga, and pay my respects to their Elders past, present, and emerging, and that the land be restored to the Aboriginal nation or nations that previously had sovereignty over the land. I extend that respect to all Aboriginal and Torres Strait Islander peoples today. I recognize this land acknowledgment is limited and engagement is an ongoing process of learning and accountability.

IT WAS LILONG WHO WANTED ME TO SEE HER. HER. MANANG AVA.

When Lilong found out that I had been accepted to study abroad in New Zealand, his first reaction was excitement over me meeting Manang Ava, his grandniece, in Australia. It seemed a convenient trip to make while living in New Zealand. Manang Ava wasn't living in that part of Australia where most people associate the Sydney Opera House or the Great Barrier Reef. She was living in a small coastal town called Dampier almost a thousand miles north of Perth, the most isolated metropolis in the world. In Dampier, kangaroos and dingoes roamed freely, Aboriginal communities were living within the horizon, and all you were surrounded by was a lush red desert with red dirt, red rocks, and an empty beach with shark cages just beyond.

I had never met Manang Ava, though I grew up knowing her as the fabled lone Valmidiano relative living in Australia where none of my other family members lived. Most of us had immigrated to the United States, particularly settling in California, Hawaii, and Washington. I knew nothing else about her except Lilong insisted I meet her. He gave me her phone number so I could call her as soon as I arrived in New Zealand.

I studied abroad in New Zealand in 1998, my junior year in college. I knew little of the country before applying, aside from what I had watched on a travel show when I was twelve-years-old — its rugged mountains, grand waterfalls, lush green hills, and first home of the commercial bungy jump. I had remained entranced with the country ever since. By the time I put in my application, I would research the history of the country's original name and residents, the Māori of Aotearoa, "Land of the Long White Cloud," whose history of colonization, discrimination, and Māori protest movement would mirror the history and struggle of Native Americans as well as the history and Civil Rights Movement of African Americans. My courses abroad focused on New Zealand Literature, Māori Politics, and the Literatures of Polynesia, Micronesia, and Melanesia.

My father wasn't thrilled. His first response: "It's too expensive." I countered that my home university sponsored the study abroad program so there would be little difference in cost. He wasn't won over, though he didn't stop me from applying and appeared surprised but also disconcerted. He might've thought I would've changed my mind when I realized the actual distance. College was two hours from home, but it didn't feel like I had moved away. I could come home any weekend I wanted, whereas New Zealand was not within reasonable distance for a quick weekend trip home.

I was used to my father not congratulating his children. He must've been secretly proud of us, but his quiet reaction to my acceptance into New Zealand was not a form of passive congratulations. He was twenty-seven when he got accepted into his first academic abroad program from the Philippines to the US, at an Ivy League no less. I was twenty when I got mine from the US to New Zealand. It seemed when my achievements surpassed the scope of his expectations, I didn't revel in any feelings of pride or joy. Rather, the feeling was relief as it felt any kind of achievement was the standard of what you were supposed to be doing all along.

Once my first semester at the University of Auckland was nearing its end, I called Manang Ava to discuss my tentative plans to see her in July during my winter break. Her voice was stern and I envisioned her to be like my paternal grandmother—frank and no-nonsense—except younger with a Filipino-Australian accent. Manang Ava asked me about the weather in Auckland, wondering if it snowed. I told her it only rained though it was freezing as there was no central heating in our apartment. She indicated it didn't snow in Dampier and their winter weather was cool. I would find out later how we each had completely different definitions of what constituted cool.

Manang Ava instructed me to fly to Karratha. When I had gone to the travel agency on campus to inquire about tickets, the travel agent had indicated there were no direct flights to Karratha but that there was a flight with two layovers leaving the next day on an exclusive student fare. The discount was ending that day and would go up by three hundred dollars tomorrow. I had to make a decision then and there. I hadn't thought about leaving tomorrow. My best friend had been with me to walk me over to the travel office. We had plans of spending a week of our winter break together, but I couldn't pass up this deal. I noticed how her face had fallen when the travel agent had said the flight was leaving tomorrow. I went ahead and booked it, much to my best friend's surprise and dismay at this sudden change of plans.

I had just moved into a flat with new flatmates the week before when I announced that I was leaving for Australia tomorrow. My flatmates and my best friend were stunned at how flippantly I could decide to travel somewhere. It seems that entire year of studying abroad was about flippant decisions.

The two layovers were in Sydney and Perth. It was the first time I had traveled completely by myself on an airplane. My flight to New Zealand from LAX didn't count as other students were with me on the same flight to Auckland. Manang Ava, nineteen years my senior, had worried about her young cousin traveling by herself.

My layover in Perth required an overnight stay before proceeding to Karratha. I had missed my connecting flight to Perth due to an arrival delay in Sydney. It was the first time I had ever missed a connecting flight. I would've felt terrified had it not been for a thirty-something Danish couple who also missed the connecting flight. Being stranded suddenly felt like no big deal.

When I finally made it on the flight across the Australian continent from Sydney to Perth, I looked at the stars through my window seat, the moon, the darkness, the Southern Cross, and cried inside as if the whole world were spinning and the plane was about to crash. But it was just me crashing as I remembered it would've been the baby's due date. I had had an abortion eight months before. Just when I thought I had forgotten, the memory had exhumed itself.

The father of said pregnancy did not like talking about it, so I never brought it up. The abortion had been four days after my twentieth birthday — Happy Birthday to me.

In the couple of months afterward, there were days when I was overwhelmed with sadness and tried discussing it with the boyfriend. He said I was making a big deal about a bunch of cells. I thought our grief was shared. I could not have been more wrong. It was not just a bunch of cells to me, but I accepted his stance and didn't argue. I grieved alone.

During my first semester abroad, I learned not to talk about my new friends or my recent adventures as the boyfriend accused me of "going out too much," "meeting too many people," "traveling too much," while he sat complacent in his upper middle-class suburb in Southern California. He had no ambitions to ever travel abroad unless his parents forced him to. We had discussed the possibility of him visiting me in New Zealand, though I would realize halfway through the year that it was just something he said to keep me hopeful.

You may ask why I didn't just break up with him. Believe me, I wanted to. Many times. But with my naïve experiences with first-kiss-first-boyfriend-first-sex and then dopamine uncontrollably surging in the brain as a result — just a love-struck, inexperienced kid craving affection — I made the very poor decision to stay in the relationship regardless of the distance between us. When I heard other people in my exchange program were in long-distance relationships with their significant others back home in California, it made me hopeful that we could stick it out. The huge difference was that their boyfriends and girlfriends visited. Mine never did.

Being wanted versus being abused was very difficult for me to differentiate between in those days. I was used to knowing them as two sides of the same coin.

Before I left for Australia, our last phone conversation somehow went off-roading into violent words delivered by him. One minute we were reminiscing and laughing about childhood friends, when out of nowhere, he made it into a contest on whose childhood friends were better. His words had felt like stones bashing my head as my eyes stung with tears and my mouth shook, stunned and speechless. He was hitting me with ridicule and violence over the phone as he attacked my childhood memories of my friends, though at twenty, I didn't define words as violent. Could words be violent? They were just words, even though they *felt* violent.

When I asked him why he started talking to me that way, he gaslit me (*gaslighting*: another term I hadn't known yet). He claimed we were just talking and why was I getting so sensitive, because obviously his childhood friends were way better than mine. I told him I was breaking up with him and then hung up. I wasn't angry. I sobbed. And I told no one as who would understand that kind of behavior and what set it off. I didn't even know. Would anyone else have known then at twenty? Could they have explained what just happened to me?

KING SIZE BED

Arriving in Perth at nearly 9 PM due to my flight delay, Manang Ava had arranged a hotel room and shuttle service. All I saw of Perth was the interior of my shuttle and my hotel room.

In Perth was the first time I ever slept in a king size bed and slept in a hotel room all by myself. It was also the first time that I had ever ordered room service. An escort service menu was placed conveniently by the dinner menu on the TV stand. Scantily clad white women in low-cut dresses, big hair, and excessive make-up sprawled throughout the menu. Curious, I flipped through each page and laughed at the thought of ordering myself a woman for dessert. Then I thought, *What kind of hotel did my cousin book me at?* I never mentioned the escort menu to her. I don't know if she had ever stayed at this hotel. It was a simple clean room with nothing to give away any nefarious activities. The bathroom was interesting. It had no tub or shower stall, but a showerhead protruding from the wall and an opaque flimsy blue shower curtain held up by metal rings on a metal circular shower rod, creating a cylindrical encasement to the tile floors.

I thought about calling the boyfriend and telling him all about the king size bed, but I had no way of calling him. I hadn't bothered purchasing an international calling card before I left Auckland. He would've only been angry at my delight. I slept in the middle of the king size bed, fully basking in the luxury.

INFANTILE AMNESIA

When I finally arrived in Karratha and was retrieving my luggage at baggage claim, I knelt down to zip up my bag and Manang Ava tapped me on the shoulder. "Are you Elsa?" I had no idea what Manang Ava looked like, though we were easy to spot as we were two of three Asians at the tiny Karratha airport. The third Asian was a Chinese girl, though Manang Ava had the sense that the young girl wasn't me. Manang Ava had curly hair which fell below her shoulders.

We were about the same height. She immediately reminded me of a younger version of my paternal grandmother just as I had guessed when I first talked to her over the phone. She possessed the same frankness that characterized the women in my family. The women of my father's side weren't meek or subtle. They were the complete opposite.

Her husband, Mac, who was a good half-foot taller than Manang Ava, drove us to their home in Dampier while I marveled at the sweeping landscape of the Pilbara. As Manang Ava had warned me earlier in a phone call, they didn't live near any big city. Deserts back home in California seemed barren with sparse flora, but the Pilbara was teeming with lush carpets of green, and its redness made the desert thrive and pop. Up until then, I realize I never looked closely at deserts back home in California to appreciate their abundance and beauty as I then stared at the Pilbara and its vast landscape before me.

Dampier is a major industrial port for the export of iron ore, liquefied natural gas, and salt. It is located about twenty minutes northwest of Karratha, in the northwest region of Western Australia. Manang Ava and her family were living there as Mac was working in the iron ore industry. The only residents on the island were the workers and their families and a very small percentage of Aboriginal families. As my two weeks would reveal, it would be a rare occurrence to cross paths with another soul.

Though modern maps show Dampier as a peninsula, Manang Ava and Mac still called it an island. They had lived there long enough to know that Dampier had once been an island until it became an artificial peninsula connected to the mainland by a highway that led to Karratha, making trips like picking up a long-lost relative from Karratha Airport, possible.

From the front passenger seat, Manang Ava remarked, "I wasn't sure how you'd look. I hadn't seen you since you were a baby." I'm sure lots of relatives held me as a baby, but she added, "I took care of you. But how could you remember?"

I knew that I had yayas, but I was never told who they had been. They were faceless young women of my infantile past who cooked, cleaned, and cared for the children. But here was Manang Ava, my former yaya, telling *me—that grown baby*—but I couldn't remember her, at least not in the adult sense that you ordinarily remember someone, and at the same time, her sudden disclosure of our yaya-alaga relationship instantly marked an affinity I innately felt toward her. Maybe this innate feeling was the memory itself finally being remembered.

HOME

At Manang Ava's home, I met her two sons—Will, seventeen, and Wes, twelve. Since I was Manang Ava's practice baby whom she fed, bathed, clothed, carried, cooed, and put to bed before she had her own babies, you could say that I was meeting my cosmic little brothers for the first time. Besides their jet-black hair and dark eyes, each brother's skin tone and eyes set their physical appearances apart. Wes took after their mother with Filipino features though had their father's eyes, while Will took after their father with fairer features though had their mother's eyes. Two large, framed photos of the brothers at much younger ages hung on the main wall of the living room. You saw them as soon as you stepped out of the foyer.

After setting my things down, I noticed the heavy metal grills on the windows and high walls in the yard. I commented on the grills when Manang Ava said they were for cyclones. It was strange to hear someone say the word, "cyclone." We called them "hurricanes" back home, but even then, we never experienced them in California. As for the high walls, she explained they were to keep the kangaroos out.

"Wow, kangaroos!"

"You've never seen a kangaroo before?" Manang Ava asked.

"We don't have them in California. We have lots of squirrels though. Have you ever seen a squirrel?"

"No," she replied.

So there, I thought. I could only guess that the prevalence of their kangaroos were the equivalent to our squirrels, though a kangaroo sighting seemed much more impressive.

"They eat kangaroos out here," Mac added.

"They?"

"Sure, restaurants and markets sell them."

"Would you like to try?" Manang Ava teased, though they both admitted they had never tried it.

I had a brief thought of what raw kangaroo meat might look like. A vision of pork ribs came to mind as I thought of kangaroo meat. To my American mindset, the kangaroo was an adorable and emblematic creature of Australia. I couldn't imagine ever eating one without thinking of it hopping around their yard. I had tried alligator meat in Auckland for the first time on a pizza, which was nothing special to me, though my eating adventures had their limitations with regards to certain animals. The kangaroo would be one of them.

As we sat down to our first dinner together, Manang Ava noticed I was sweating. Concerned, she asked if I was hot and if I'd like to have the A/C turned on.

"Yes, please!" I replied, instantly relieved that they had A/C. "I wasn't expecting it to be this hot when you said it was going to be cool in Dampier. This is hot for winter weather."

The current temperature did not feel hot to them. Manang Ava noted how summers got so hot that the wax of their candles would be completely melted by the time they returned from long trips out-of-town.

FAMILY TREE

Over dinner, Manang Ava explained how we were related. As it was with many relatives, I didn't know how we were related. The relation was oftentimes through a great- or great-great-grandparent so far up the tree that my generation was not very diligent about tracing. Manang Ava explained we were the great-granddaughters of Pedro and Petrona from the tiny Ilocano barrio Labnig, in the town of Lapog. Their sons were our paternal grandfathers. Her father was Lilong's nephew and my father's first cousin.

As I would learn from Manang Ava, Lilong had been extremely close to her father as her father had become estranged from his own father. The reasons behind the estrangement were never made clear, though Lilong had stepped in as father figure to his nephew, which made me recall my closeness to Lilong and the periods of conflict with my own father.

When Lilong suspected that I was having a hard time with my father, he had told me plainly in English, one of the only times he had spoken to me in English outside of his usual

Ilocano, "If you ever have a problem with your father, you talk to me and I'll take care of it. Okay?"

Lilong was matter-of-fact in that moment, unlike the tender and light-hearted way he usually expressed himself. I must've been eighteen at the time, fighting my way to become a Literature major when my father couldn't see why I couldn't be an Engineer like my two older siblings. I was on the verge of tears when I received Lilong's kind offer. Lilong had just wrapped up his usual afternoon tending to our expansive fruit and vegetable garden in our backyard. We were both buckled in my car. I was driving him home.

I could've told him so much in that moment—the profanity that his son hurled at us if we made a mistake or weren't achieving to his standards—but I couldn't involve him. I can imagine what my grandfather would've said to his own son, but I could also see it backfiring. My father had a way of taking his rage out on his other children when he couldn't direct it at me, pitting my siblings against me so they blamed me for our father's outbursts. I thought Lilong must've been keenly aware of his son's relentless disposition toward his children, and I decided it was best to not make Lilong the cause of my father never speaking to me again.

My father's demands for academic excellence had reached a breaking point. His way of pushing us did not necessarily lead to academic excellence but to suicidal ideation or self-harm.

Two decades later, my aunt, who was equally not immune from suicidal ideation or self-harm throughout her life, would reveal to me how Lilong had beaten her with a slipper for her refusal to take her college typewriting exam, a requirement to graduate college then. She didn't think she could pass. A typewriting exam may seem trivial, but for my aunt, it was one of the very steps to get out of the barrio, because in order to work in an office and not a rice paddy, you had to know how to type.

My aunt's long-buried information colored my long-standing view of Lilong, and at the same time, it didn't. I knew, as well as anybody in my family, that he had wanted a better life for his children, which meant leaving the barrio for good. He didn't want his children or his descendants to ever work knee deep in rice paddies again.

Likewise, my own father wanted the very best for us. He had made huge sacrifices for our education and privileged lives, but it oftentimes felt that it was more so to reflect the best parts of himself, which I think he felt people didn't recognize enough. We were to be an ongoing reflection of all that the lowly boy from the barrio had achieved but it would be at the expense of our own emotional and mental wellbeing. He refused to see that we were people too, not clay figures he could command at will. His encouragement for the things he saw as worthy could be cloaked in a gentle voice and then whose imperiousness could unleash words that gutted the marrow from your bones.

In hindsight, I still appreciated Lilong's kind offer to intervene between me and my father, despite the fact that my father's parenting style probably mirrored what he had learned growing up. Minus the slipper, my father preferred words.

The heroism and closeness I had long attached to my own relationship with Lilong must've mirrored the closeness between Manang Ava's father and Lilong, which naturally spilled down to the children, and so Lilong had somehow become Manang Ava's own Lilong.

Manang Ava went on to explain her additional closeness to my grandmother. I thought the affection toward Lilang had occurred by default due to being close to Lilong, but Manang Ava revealed how the closeness to Lilang was actually biological. Her paternal grandmother was Lilang's first cousin. Thus, Manang Ava was not only related to me through my grandfather but also my grandmother. I did not ask her then to delve into the specifics. I had a hard time wrapping my head around it.

My father, twenty-three years later, would explain it to me in simple terms: Imagine two brothers who married two girls, but the girls were first cousins. That was how Manang Ava was related to me on both my paternal grandparents' sides. Her paternal grandmother's mother was sister to my paternal grandmother's father. Thus, our paternal grandmothers were first cousins while our paternal grandfathers were brothers. Even the girl cousins' nicknames were very similar—Atang and Arang—that one could become easily confused.

Manang Ava never met her grandmother, so Lilang became her connection to the grandmother she never knew.

"Lilong Tito and Lilang Atang lived next door to us in Labnig. When I was a little girl, I would sleep over and your Lilang would tell me stories about my Lilang. I wondered how she knew my grandmother so well. 'She is my cousin,' she told me. Your Lilang Atang is a sweet lady."

Manang Ava's description seemed at odds with what I had come to know about Lilang. She had witnessed moments when Lilang would become passive depending on who the person was. Maybe Lilong? Maybe someone else whom she thought was in a position of authority? Though Lilang spoiled me and my little sister—her two youngest granddaughters—some family members would've greatly contested Manang Ava's generous description of Lilang. We can have such conflicting views about one another that it's hard to know who is telling the truth. Maybe we all were.

I remember the usual afternoon visit at my grandparents' house. Lilang had poked fun at my short skirt "nakiting ti paldam" and red lipstick. I didn't think my skirt very short and I didn't think my lipstick very red, but she smirked. She never said, "You can't wear that." Instead she found it amusing that her academically stellar sixteen-year-old granddaughter would wear short skirts and red lipstick. The memory of that mischievous smirk still amuses me twenty-five years later.

Meanwhile, both my aunts' accounts of Lilang present a stark difference to the easy-going, easily amused woman whom I had grown up with. As a mother, Lilang expected her daughters to take care of her, forgoing any opportunity of marriage and children. One daughter obeyed. The other did not. While the second daughter was seen as disobedient in her mother's eyes, she went on to become an accomplished career woman, wife, and mother. Then there was my father, the favored eldest son, who seemed to have done everything right according to Lilang—handsome, an Ivy League graduate, and marrying a beautiful Ilocana virgin.

I imagine how the relationship between each child and their mother gravely affected how the siblings treated each other.

Or maybe I am projecting the divisions within my own sibling relationships when it came to our father.

CRUSH

Manang Ava had set me up in Wes' room while Wes shared Will's room. Wes was into Baby Spice of the Spice Girls with various pictures of her all along his bedroom wall though I am pretty sure Wes cared little for the Spice Girls or their music. As fate would have it, a future Wes and his future wife—beautiful but with gorgeous brunette hair, far from resembling his twelve-year-old dream of Baby Spice—would eventually be rock musicians whose musical inspirations would include bands like Rage Against the Machine. However, I would forever remember Baby Spice as a twelve-year-old's mad crush on the blonde-haired, pink-accessorized, doe-eyed girlish beauty, Emma Bunton.

In this unfettered display of Wes' celebrity crush on his walls, my father would've discouraged such a display, as if his children's stellar academic achievements could eliminate any physical desires we might have had. My mother was the same. Crushes and boys were stricken into silence, but it didn't mean they didn't exist. They were simply never discussed. And thus, we learned not to ever display or mention it in front of our parents.

And so Baby Spice, with her long blonde pigtails, frayed blonde bangs, big blue eyes, and big wide smile, was the first thing that greeted me every morning and the last thing I saw before falling asleep.

WES

In stark contrast to Auckland's cold and rainy winter, a Dampier winter averaged with highs of 80 to 85 degrees during my stay. Evenings never required a sweater.

Manang Ava had assigned Wes to show me around Dampier the next morning.

Wes and I walked side by side along the beach without saying much to each other. He showed me where I could swim and run and what part of Dampier I should avoid, where the iron ore and salt workers, mostly men, congregated.

"You're almost as tall as me," I said, when he broke out of his shyness to stand on his tippy-toes to make himself taller than me. I laughed and thought, *Here is the cute little brother I never had.* Wes' features were very "Valmidiano." The hue of his skin was undoubtedly Filipino. I imagined my father must've looked like Wes when he was twelve.

We sat on rocks along the shore when Wes pointed out East Intercourse Island. To the right was another tiny island with an oasis of palm trees. Wes told me the story of a hermit who lived there. I didn't remember much about the hermit's story except that I stared at the palm trees surrounding the lonely shack, barely discernible in the distance. I wondered if Wes was just passing along Dampier lore or if it was true.

Twenty-three years later, in the midst of writing this piece, Wes would confirm the hermit story, sending me an article of the man, Sam Ostojich, a Serbian immigrant, and his pet cat, Tiger, who resided on Tidepole Island, though the island would be affectionately named after him—Sam's Island. He retired on the island when landholder Rio Tinto granted him a lifelong lease after he was injured in an accident. He lived there alone with his oasis of palm trees, which he lovingly maintained through his own irrigation system. The island's structures and palm trees would ultimately fall into disrepair after his death in 2005.

The Pilbara landscape, though desert to the metropolitan eye, was stunning with its red dirt, red rocks, carpets of green, and blue water. I could see other islands in the distance. It was the first time the Indian Ocean was at my feet. When I'd be on a beach in New Zealand, I'd wave across the Pacific, imagining the boyfriend at the other end of it. But with the Indian Ocean before me, I could not wave to the boyfriend as he was facing the wrong direction.

Top: to the right in the distance is Sam's Island with his oasis of palm trees
Bottom: The Pilbara landscape, 1998

The Dampier Archipelago was formed approximately eight thousand years ago when rising sea levels flooded the coastal plains. The prominent rock features of the area are among the oldest in the world, formed three billion years ago.

Dampier takes its name from the British pirate William Dampier, who explored the north and west coasts of Australia in 1688 and 1699. He is lauded as the first Englishman to set foot in Australia and published a popular book with a derogatory description of Aboriginal people that would influence the foundations of Australia. Dr. Dawn Casey, an Aboriginal descendant of the Tagalaka clan from Croydon would explain how William Dampier's racism and the influence his words had on the perspectives of Captain James Cook and Joseph Banks and those governors that came after who employed academics and anthropologists, had undoubtedly set the blueprint for Aboriginal Australia, judging Aboriginal people for the perception of failing to meet European measures of sophistication.

British colonization had marked the beginning of a destruction of an Aboriginal way of life despite their existence on the continent for tens of thousands of years.

I would learn Australia's brutal history of Stolen Children, rape, disease, land seizure, and particularly the Flying Foam Massacre of the Burrup Peninsula. Until now, written word about the massacre—which white men love to rely on the written word—would remain scarce, except Aboriginal men and women would pass the story on to their children, grandchildren, and great-grandchildren, who would hold the story, generation after generation, inside their blood, bones, and mouths—of their maternal ancestor raped by white men, their paternal ancestor tortured while forced to watch, the protective retaliation of the Aboriginal community to avenge their harmed members, and the ultimate annihilation of nearly their entire ancestral community by white men who feel vindicated to destroy a people whom they feel beneath them. It's an unwritten story too many of us know, in different lands among different peoples, where white men today still do not believe the history unless it's written down, where intergenerational emotional scars on the Black and Brown dispossessed Body do not count.

As Jade Kennedy, a Yuin leader from the Illawarra and South Coast of New South Wales, would remark in the 21st century, "When we welcome people into our country, we're welcoming you into our home. The brother's responsibility now is to acknowledge that welcome."

Manang Ava and Mac had discussed Australian politics, educating me on Pauline Hanson who advocated anti-immigration sentiment against Asians. Throughout her political career which continues to a senatorial position today, she would continue to make racial inflammatory statements in demeaning speeches and propose racist legislation, blasting Australian Aboriginal people as "lazy" and "negligent" and claiming, "billions have gone to the non-productive, unrepentant Aboriginal industry."

William Dampier's legacy lives on.

The five Traditional Custodian groups of the area are Ngarluma, Yaburara, Mardudhunera, Yindjibarndi, and Wong-Goo-Tt-Oo, collectively known as Ngarda-Ngarli. The peninsula's true name is Murujuga, which means "Hip Bone Sticking Out" in the Ngarluma-Yaburara language, and refers to the forty-two islands of the Dampier Archipelago and the Burrup Peninsula. The Ngarda-Ngarli have been part of Murujuga for at least fifty thousand years and have a deep and spiritual connection to the land.

Murujuga is home to one of the largest and most diverse collections of rock art in the world with more than one million images. The petroglyphs capture at least 47,000 years of human existence and provide an archaeological record of traditional use of the area. It has deep meaning for the Ngarda-Ngarli, providing a tangible link to stories, customs, and knowledge of their land and resources and connecting them to the events and people of the past and their beliefs today. Ngarda-Ngarli people say ancestral beings created the land during the Dreamtime, i.e., when the Earth was soft, and the spirits of Ngkurr, Bardi and Gardi continue to live in the area. They left their mark in features like the Marntawarrura, or "black hills," said to be stained with their creative blood.

In my own Motherland, each region has their own origin story of how certain volcanoes, lakes, hills, islands, and oceans came to be in our archipelago of over seven thousand islands. Before Spanish colonization, the entire Ilocos region where my parents and ancestors are from, was originally called Samtoy, a contraction of "Sao mi ditoy" which means "Our language here" in Ilocano. We have gods and spirits, too. Aran and Angalo were our colossal parents who created the Earth.

I wondered if the ancestral beings of Murujuga felt my presence and were curious, or maybe they weren't as they had seen Wes, a familiar face who looked like me. With Brown skin.

As Wes and I strolled through Dampier, there was no one around to observe though I imagine I must've been easy to spot as I was Brown and small. I was now someone to be looked at.

Before traveling to New Zealand and Australia, I never thought I was one to be looked at. Except for my short height, I had looked like any other Filipino girl in my predominantly Filipino Catholic elementary school in the LA suburbs. But now amidst the sweeping red desert of Dampier island, I didn't see myself in anyone else except Manang Ava and her two boys.

As my eyes scanned the horizon, I wondered where the Aboriginal communities might be while I don't think anyone in Dampier wondered about my existence or my origins.

COMPLETELY ALONE

I asked Manang Ava later that afternoon if it was safe for me to go running by myself. "Why wouldn't it?" she wondered. When I jokingly asked if it was okay for me to run at midnight, she didn't bat an eyelash and replied, "Yes," though wondered why anyone would want to run at midnight.

I chose to run at sunset until it was completely dark, something I had never done before by myself. In America, women are taught to never walk alone at night as you ran the risk of rape or assault. But in Murujuga, no such dangers existed.

The freedom of running alone at night was exhilarating.

I ran along the beach where Wes and I had walked earlier. I watched the sky turn a fiery orange. The sun had set behind East Intercourse Island, illuminating the water with an eerie red glow. There would be silence except for the sound of my own breath and my feet hitting the pavement.

My thoughts wandered to my parents and siblings in California when I spotted a wild dog in the dark, strolling toward me. Afraid it was a dingo, and only knowing them to eat babies as I had popularly associated them growing up, I backtracked the way I came. I ran three complete laps, running along the beach and then to a football field where the floodlights illuminated my path, and I'd run up and over, circling the corner.

On another evening, I spied a mama kangaroo and her baby, standing upright, side by side on the beach, watching the sunset. From afar, they looked like a mother and child with large tails. As I came closer, I saw their silhouettes on the beach and wished I had my camera to capture such a magical moment.

FOURTH OF JULY

On my third day in Dampier, it was the Fourth of July. I forgot it was a holiday until it was about noon when Will noted the date. I didn't let anyone know what a big holiday it was—the fireworks and BBQs and cheesy displays of American patriotism with people waving their flags on their lawns and wearing red, white, and blue. Instead, I watched TV, the only time I watched TV during my entire two weeks in Dampier.

I watched an episode of *Days of Our Lives* with Manang Ava. Dampier was many years behind on *Days of Our Lives*, though the episodes they aired were all new to her.

I watched Will Smith and Martin Lawrence's *Bad Boys* on videocassette with Will and Wes. They were surprised I had never seen it.

They only had two channels in Dampier. When I told them that Americans could have as many as one hundred channels, Will and Wes were flabbergasted.

"What could you possibly watch on a hundred channels?" Will asked.

A lot of garbage.

TO MARKET, TO MARKET

In the afternoon, Manang Ava and Mac drove to Karratha with their kids and me in tow. They made the drive at least once a month to stock up on food and supplies. My stay happened to fall on such a day. My shampoo and conditioner bottles of Salon Selectives were running low. I couldn't live without its strawberry smelling fragrance. I wondered if they even carried the brand in Karratha.

Aside from walking around the island, laying out on the beach, swimming, running in the evenings, or staring at the Pilbara landscape, the trip to the store in Karratha was another adventure.

On the drive to Karratha, I had asked Manang Ava and Mac how they met and how long did they date before they got married. Mac, in the driver's seat, laughed and said, "We just got married." Without either of them elaborating, I replied, "Oh." It seemed to be a long story that they were both saving for later.

At the market, Manang Ava went shopping for groceries. Mac and Wes went in search of fishing tackle. Will helped me find my bottles of Salon Selectives. Will found the bottles though I noticed the packaging looked slightly different and their fragrance wasn't as strawberry-fragrant as I was used to in California. When Will asked how it smelled, I flipped the cap open and let him take a whiff.

"Fruity and sweet," he remarked.

The cashier, an Aboriginal woman in a pressed magenta uniform, rang up my shampoo and conditioner. I delighted in hearing her accent. Her dark wavy hair with copper tint was tied up in a thick bun. Her eyes looked weary after what I guessed was a long day. I must've had a stupid grin on my face when she glanced at me quizzically as I said, "Thank you" in my American accent.

After regrouping with Manang Ava, Mac, and Wes, we headed off into the parking lot when an Aboriginal boy of about nine or ten-years-old, who stood at my height with strikingly cornsilk blond tousled hair, had walked into the market with a man whom I assumed was his father. The man's hair was not blond but was dark brown and equally tousled. Both were dressed in tattered knee-length denim shorts, and both walked in with their bare feet dusted with the desert. The boy had no shirt as his thin torso was also finely dusted with the desert. His father wore a faded checkered-blue, button-down, short-sleeve shirt. I then thought of the "NO SHIRT NO SHOES NO SERVICE" signs hanging up in Starbucks windows at Hermosa Beach in Southern California where I lived. They had no such signs in Karratha shop windows. The boy and I briefly looked at each other as we passed. I marveled at his strikingly cornsilk blond tousled hair. He may have briefly marveled at me, this five-foot girl with straight long black hair and tan skin, not as dark as his, but whose likeness was never seen about their parts. One, two seconds, of marveling at each other. I suppose we both wondered where each of the other lived.

CAR KEYS

As we packed into the car, I was surprised when Mac handed Manang Ava the keys.

"You're driving?" I asked. I realize how that question might've sounded.

"Of course," Manang Ava replied, with a tinge of annoyance in her voice.

"I drove here, and she can drive back," Mac said.

"He's tired, so yes, I'm driving," Manang Ava added.

I immediately thought of my parents. My mother never drove with my father as a passenger. Though my mother did drive, and would drive herself and her children around, my father was the driver when it was between them in a car. When I came to think of it, I didn't know many women in my circle who drove when their husbands were in the car. When it came between a husband and wife in a car, it seemed the husband always drove. My mother did not drive freeways or pump her own gas. My father's eldest sister drove the freeway and pumped her own gas, but she was forever single, which warranted that she had no choice but to do these things herself. Growing up under my mother, I had received the impression that women of my parents' cultural generation were seen as meek damsels, not tough enough to perform certain tasks no matter how mundane or trivial those tasks might've been—like driving the freeway, pumping your own gas, or driving your husband around as a passenger.

I was quietly filled with awe as Manang Ava drove us home.

JUST GOT MARRIED

Once the dinner plates were cleared and washed, Manang Ava and Mac shared their love story and how they ended up in Dampier. It was time for Manang Ava and Mac to elaborate on Mac's earlier statement that he had made in the car on our way to Karratha: "We just got married."

Their love had started with letters.

Before the meretricious business of being able to order yourself a Filipina bride online, the Philippines had long been in the business of putting ads in their local newspapers, requesting young, unmarried women to become pen pals to young men overseas. Manang Ava wasn't even the one who had started the letter-writing to her now husband, though she was no stranger to the letter-writing business.

A year or two before writing her husband, Manang Ava had gotten involved in a long love-letter-affair with a young Filipino officer overseas. She didn't think him very handsome and never took their love letters seriously. Over two years, she and the young officer had written long letters to each other. In one final letter, he had proposed marriage. Manang Ava, though flattered and surprised, refused. She had never met this man and couldn't commit to someone whom she had never met. She had enjoyed writing letters and receiving them but admitted the relationship didn't seem real. Manang Ava had replied with her rejection, breaking the young man's heart and never heard from him again. She didn't intend to enter the business of writing another love letter to a man she would never meet.

Love letters to Mac began with her sister who pretended to be Manang Ava in the initial letters. Whether the intention was to find Manang Ava a husband or not, the business of letter-writing itself seemed the young ladies' way of innocent entertainment without the repercussions of what a real-life passionate love affair could bring. It must've been nice to feel adored by a man bearing his soul to you—all emotional attachments laid completely bare in words—but without the pressures of physical intimacy that could lead to carnal acts not fit for a Filipina where society demanded her virginity until marriage.

Mac had been living and working in Papua New Guinea then. He was originally from Australia but worked in the iron ore industry. He had lived in an isolated bachelor society, which afforded none of the men any female companionship they longed for. Whether it was his iron ore employer or himself who placed the ad in a Philippine newspaper to start a correspondence, or whether it was an interesting thing he wrote or a handsome photograph he sent, it wasn't long before Manang Ava took over the letter-writing from her sister, the baton successfully passed, and once again the business of love letter-writing began with a man whom she didn't think she would ever meet.

Over a year or two, the pair wrote, and at the bottom of each letter, Manang Ava signed her name formally with an x next to her name, and then underlined it like a signature block. Mac matched her signature but with lots of x's. XXXXXX. When Ava received his letters, she was puzzled by his many x's and wondered why he had written so many. As the two recall these love letters, Mac laughs about the x's.

Unlike the Filipino officer, Mac did not propose marriage in a letter. Instead, when time off from the iron ore business presented itself, he booked a flight to the Philippines. With no plan except to meet the girl he had fallen in love with through their love letters, Mac had hailed down a cab at the

Manila airport. From the backseat, he simply said, "Take me here," pointing to the address on the envelope—the same address that had appeared on every envelope she had ever written him.

There was no warning he was showing up on her doorstep. He never wrote that he was. He just showed up. However, he didn't show up on her doorstep as immediately as he had wanted as the cab driver had driven him all over Manila for a few hours to drive up the meter for the white man in his cab. Mac, fed up with being driven literally all over town, finally demanded to be delivered to the address on his envelope.

The address on the envelope was that of my aunt in Quezon City. Manang Ava had been living with my aunt, completing her midwife degree—a degree she had no interest in but one that her family thought would be a stable career. She would later admit to me that childbirth, outside of the birth of her own two children, was not something she found amazing. She admitted she found it "gross."

Upon seeing Mac on her doorstep, Manang Ava swore it was love at first sight. The man from her love letters was real. She thought he was the most handsome man she had ever seen, and here he was, on her doorstep. He had flown all the way from Papua New Guinea to meet her.

Manang Ava asked me quite breathlessly, "Have you seen his picture when he was young?" I could only guess she was referring to an 8 x 10 framed photograph perched on an end table next to the sofa in the living room, what I could only suspect was their "We Just Got Married" photo—a petite Ava and her beautiful Brown skin with thin arms and a curly bob haircut, primped in a late 1970s white short-sleeve mini dress, standing next to her tall, white, hottie husband with blond hair, equally groomed in a white short-sleeve button-down dress shirt that closely resembled the Filipino barong.

For the next day or two, Manang Ava was not allowed to be alone with Mac. Constantly surrounded by an entourage of relatives, particularly my aunt, Mac and Ava could not get to know each other. She would say nothing while our aunt would dominate conversation and speak on Manang Ava's behalf as if she had no voice of her own. Finally, while touring around town, Mac took Ava's hand and told my aunt, "I don't want to talk to *you*. I want to talk to *her*." And with that, he stole Ava away to a place where they could talk and get to know each other. It was after that, literally right after that, "We just got married."

Thus, Mac went to the Philippines a single man. He left the Philippines a married man.

Without delay, Ava joined Mac in PNG where she found it weird how her new white husband's friends liked to drink too much while her new white husband's friends found it weird how Mac's new Filipina wife liked to eat mangoes with salt. For the first few years, they lived in a gated house where the neighborhood guards would stare at her. No one else in the vicinity looked like her. She felt uncomfortable being watched. Driving around town, she recounted seeing women nursing their baby with one breast and then nursing a piglet with the other—baby and piglet both cradled in the woman's arms as if it were the most normal occurrence on the street. Ava had never seen anything like it.

Rock pianist Tori Amos came to mind as I thought of her 1996 *Boys For Pele* album and her album sleeve photo of herself nursing a sleeping piglet with her left breast, her blouse unbuttoned, and the center of her bare chest exposed while tenderly cradling the piglet in her arms as she would a human baby. The public reaction to the photo—horror, disgust, perplexity. All of the above. I had no strong aversion seeing Tori nurse a piglet—it was Tori Amos after all, Tori was Tori, and I was used to her provocative images on her albums. However, Manang Ava's up-close and personal observation of a PNG woman nursing a piglet right before her eyes was not met with the same nonchalance. "Pigs are the same worth as humans there," Manang Ava clicked her tongue.

It was during those early years of marriage in PNG that Manang Ava was lonely but credits her mother-in-law for giving her the courage to speak up for herself when she was pregnant with her firstborn. At her first prenatal appointment, the doctor didn't think Manang Ava understood English. Having been raised in the Philippines where she was used to elders speaking on her behalf or speaking over her, it was her mother-in-law who encouraged her to speak up for herself. "Speak up, love," she would encourage, "Tell the doctor."

After a few years, Mac secured an iron ore post in Dampier where Manang Ava and their two sons relocated. Free from the confines of a gated home, Manang Ava now had the freedom to roam about with no guards watching her every move. Mac and Manang Ava had planned to live in Dampier until Mac's retirement, and then they would finally move to Queensland to live out the rest of their days.

Despite their isolation in Dampier, Manang Ava made sure her boys knew their Filipino heritage by taking them home to the Philippines for visits so that the country was not some far off land but a part of their identity and experience too.

Throughout her marriage, Manang Ava was a proud stay-at-home mom—something both my parents frowned upon when it came to their own daughters' futures, preferring their daughters work but also cook and clean for their husbands as was expected of a good wife, despite the fact that we might be working the same amount or twice as hard as our husbands. My little sister would join the ranks of Manang Ava and defy my parents' wishes as she saw the value in staying home to raise each of her five children before eventually returning to the workforce.

Manang Ava was far from the passive spouse. From her, I learned an alternative view of what marriage could look like, different than what I had seen in my own parents' marriage.

SACRED SINS

Once Mac and Manang Ava reached the end of their happily-ever-after, and Mac had since gone to bed, Manang Ava unexpectedly broke open silences that my family never talked about. She broke them open as if she were recounting information I already knew, but how could I have known?

She began to tell me about my family's life in the Philippines when I was a baby — our life before we immigrated to the United States. Manang Ava was my yaya, you see, a fact I never knew until she told me. My parents had gone through a slew of unreliable yayas, so my parents were very grateful when they could employ the help of Manang Ava, my father's niece.

By twenty-years-old, Manang Ava was already running my parents' house and caring for three small children—my six-year-old brother, my four-year-old sister, and me, an infant. On top of that, she was earning a degree in midwifery. She made my life at twenty, despite all of its personal struggles and trauma and stress, look like a walk in the park.

"Your mum spoke Ilocano and Tagalog so elegantly. She could switch between the two easily. When she did cook, her cooking was the best. And she was always reading."

I imagine my beautiful young mother — the career woman and occasional chef — sitting by the window under the sunlight, reading a novel undisturbed.

Manang Ava told me stories of my older siblings when they were young. How they used to wait up for my mother when she worked late nights in Metro Manila. How they would not eat dinner until she came home, which could sometimes be as late as 9 PM as my mother faced a long commute. My father had been working overseas on an environmental project for the United Nations. My older sister would wait at the dinner table every night, refusing to eat, and refusing to get ready for bed, until she saw my mother. Manang Ava tried cooking meals my four-year-old sister might like, but my sister just couldn't eat dinner without my mother.

Manang Ava told me stories of how my father used to sit his four-year-old and six-year-old down in serious conference, discussing college and careers. Children were but little adults to my parents, who could grasp the meaning of bigger issues in the world. Nothing was too complex for their children to grasp no matter what age.

As Manang Ava told me these stories, she wondered what my childhood must've been like under such a father. She reiterated stories of the same old, tired advice that he gave her as he had given me time and time again. As my yaya, she had lived under my parents' roof for a brief time. Manang Ava was fifteen years younger than my father. It seems my father felt the need to take on the role of an authoritative father figure in her life. Manang Ava didn't always agree with his advice, just like I didn't, though for Manang Ava to disagree was a trailblazing thing for a woman of her time. At one point, my father tried setting her up with his ginger-haired, balding, white friend from work. "He's bald and he's old," she said. No one defied my father, and yet Manang Ava bravely, and unfalteringly, did.

She relayed these intimate details about our daily lives that my infantile amnesia did not afford me to remember, and here she served these unremembered memories as if on a buffet platter. She shared stories she probably shouldn't have even told me. She brought up sacred sins.

I only called them "sacred" as they were the past sins of elders which the younger generation was never supposed to know. Such sins were to be forever silenced and hopefully forgotten. They were the sins committed by men in our family—the possible rapes and molestations—though Manang Ava never used the word "rape" or "molest," but the word "touch" as if to soften the blow, as if there were ambiguity in the consent of touch itself, where the victim is not a victim but a participant.

I think of the little girls who grew into women.

I think of all the sins these women held, not even theirs but they held them, never breaking, or at least not that I ever saw.

I imagine the breaking happened behind closed doors. Childhood and adolescent observations of unexplained tears, unexplained mood swings, unexplained withdrawals from any social interaction with family members, the unexpected cold shoulders and then the sudden wanting to connect again.

I didn't know how to tell Manang Ava that the sudden and unexpected unloading of all this information made me uncomfortable. I didn't know how to say that these sacred sins should never have been sacred in the first place. I didn't know how to say that it was never that little girl or young woman's fault.

The tyranny of forefathers could still persist, enabled by descendant silencing, where a painful past is better left unremembered. Silence, as I learned from my parents, equated to the perfect appearance of our supposedly perfect little families.

Where one-time affairs with teenage girls were neither "one time" nor "affairs," I wondered if they were frightened young girls who were tricked, cornered, and raped by much older powerful men in the barrio, though family history would rewrite them as "mistresses" or simply women of the normalized querida culture, where powerful men were expected and accepted to sate their sexual appetites outside of their marriage with precocious girls. These forefathers who flaunted their conquests, facing little consequence and little complaint from their obedient wives. Marriage and its sanctity were but an empty, meaningless title. The possession of a querida or two were like little side hustles that added to the "wealth" of a man—a special badge to flaunt among the old boys colonizers' club. There was always someone else's uncle or grandfather who had a second family, and maybe even a third.

I would eventually learn that we as a people were not always like this.

I would learn how the querida culture—as derived from the Spanish word, *querida*—was not a cultural practice that was originally ours but was put in place by white colonizers who destroyed societies held together under the authority of high priestesses, comprised of women and gender-fluid individuals, and replaced them with their patriarchal structure. Male descendants would fail to honor the spirit of our matriarchal ancestors and instead adopt the ways of the colonizer as if using women were the proper way to prove a man's worth. Some Filipino descendants would argue in defense of these patriarchs, "But those were just the times," when the truth is that it was not always "the times."

There were also families separated by migration. My parents, aunts, and uncles didn't talk about them either. Outside of the children's knowledge, husbands had left wives behind in the barrio to work as menial laborers, Sakadas, and longshoremen in the United States from the early 1900s to the 1940s, sending remittances Home to ensure their families' survival, though there is no mention of how wives could not be petitioned to join their husbands then.

The United States had seized control over our islands after the Spanish and had been set against Filipinos forming families on US soil by limiting the immigration of women from our archipelago. While few Filipina women were able to migrate, the passage of the American Page Act, passed by an all white male governing body, had restricted anyone of Asian descent on the pretense of barring "lewd and immoral purposes." Women of Asian descent were erroneously affiliated with prostitution at the time rather than seen as seeking a better life with their husband and family. Decades and decades would go by. Filipino husbands eventually remarried in the US, while descendants didn't dare understand why husbands and wives couldn't stay faithful to each other with an entire ocean between them for a lifetime.

Divorce has never been legal in the Philippines, where it was expected that abandoned wives stay chaste and never remarry even though their husbands overseas had the freedom to do so. The first wife with her first children never talked about it, as if these second families overseas didn't exist.

This history of fragmented families and broken marriages would take shape in shame and silence a century later, as if our ancestors had the complete wherewithal to control the course of their lives within the confines of American law.

Great-granddaughters would continue to be held to the same expectation of propriety, and if they didn't, were told they had become "too American."

Now here was Manang Ava, a sequestered witness on the continent of Australia. Silence to any and all family secrets of the past that had once been an automatic given was now being shattered as I was in Manang Ava's sequestered space.

She had nothing to lose in breaking open the silence. Who would tell her that she wasn't supposed to?

The code of silence I grew up knowing wasn't relevant in Australia.

WILL

For three straight days, I went swimming by myself. My pale, winter skin became tan in a matter of days. Manang Ava remarked how quickly I darkened.

The only people I passed on the beach had been on the first day. A man and his young daughter, about seven-years-old, was dragging her large puppy, whom she called, "Bear! Come on, Bear!" She giggled as her dog, a German Shepherd, jumped on me and wriggled around in the sand. The little girl was wearing a short wetsuit with pink stripes on the side and a dark blue baseball cap that hid her blonde hair tied up in a ponytail. Father and daughter were both white but deeply tanned by the Murujuga sun.

"Ya plan to go swimming?" the father asked me. "The water is deepest if you keep walking south," he pointed.

In the distance, two teenage girls swam and squealed in their turquoise and blue swimsuits. I decided to stop where I was and swim where I felt the water did not go past five feet. I was all alone. It was not the kind of beach that ever had a lifeguard on duty. Manang Ava warned me of shark cages and recommended that I not swim too far. The water was so shallow that as I swam out farther and farther, barely seeing my towel on the sand, I could still stand in the water that rose up as far as my chin.

At the end of my first week, I invited Will and Wes to go swimming with me. Sadly, Wes developed a cold and was ordered by Manang Ava to stay home. He was confined to Will's room with the humidifier on. The root of Wes' cold was puzzling as I wondered how anyone could get sick in the midst of their extremely warm weather. I realize now how my request to have the A/C on during my stay was probably the root of Wes' cold as the family never used the A/C at this time of year. While it felt like summer to me, it was still their winter. An 85-degree climate felt comfortable and cool to them. They were used to scorching temperatures of over a hundred degrees during their summer, which would then warrant the use of the A/C. Over two decades later, I would regret how my spoiled Americanness had made my poor twelve-year-old Australian nephew sick.

Leaving Wes behind, I took Will swimming. His fair skin had tanned for what seemed the first time in a very long time. His mother was shocked to see the color of her son's skin upon our return for dinner.

As Will and I swam out, he told me of his recent make-out adventures, how he had attempted to give a girl a hickey, but her skin was so pale that it barely turned any color no matter how much he sucked on her neck. I laughed though refrained from telling him any of my sexual misadventures.

During one afternoon when I resumed swimming alone and decided to swim out further than I had before, jellyfish surrounded me as I popped my head up a quarter of a mile away from shore. Miraculously I was never stung. My swimming days in Murujuga were numbered. It was no longer safe to swim or walk on the sand with the invasion of jellyfish that littered the beach by the hundreds.

In the late afternoon for the next few days, Will and I would walk along the beach where hundreds of jellyfish had beached themselves, a site of an eerie mass suicide. I asked Will if this jellyfish invasion was normal. He didn't say it was, though his seventeen-year-old self didn't seem to notice or care very much. It was nothing I had ever seen. Their fragile luminescence shimmered under the sun. They lay in the sand, defeated, with no way back into the water. Would they shrivel or disappear, or would the ocean surreptitiously snatch them back during the night? The tide had pulled back dramatically leaving more jellyfish stranded in the afternoons.

Will and I did a photo shoot around the rocks by the beach. I slipped on wet rocks in my bare feet, landing on my back. I didn't sustain any bruises, though slipping and falling in front of Will felt more embarrassing than anything else. I laughed while on my back staring at the sky. Will ran to my rescue and helped me up.

Photo shoot where I slipped on wet rocks in my bare feet
Dampier, 1998

We made a stop at the small tourist shop atop a low hill. The tourist shop was dark with no windows. Will and I were the only ones inside. An older white woman with thick glasses and short gray hair had been working behind the counter and didn't seem cognizant of our presence as we browsed around the store. She continued to focus on her paperwork. Did anyone else ever come in? Though the landscape and beaches were stunning, Murujuga did not seem to attract tourists, or maybe I came at the wrong time of year.

I browsed the beautiful didgeridoos on display. They had intricate hand-carved and hand-painted Aboriginal designs on them, but I had no intention of buying one. Some were as big if not bigger than me. I had my eye on an adorable stuffed wombat that I was thinking about getting for my little sister. Will dissuaded me, seeing no point in buying a stuffed animal. When I thought about it, the adorable stuffed wombat was not worth stuffing into my suitcase.

As we exited the store and were back in the afternoon sun, we were steps away from a vista point where I stopped to take more pictures of the red rocks peeking amidst pockets of green that swept across the Pilbara when Will spotted a kangaroo. He signaled me to hush as we crept close, and I tried to take snapshots. In contrast to the silhouetted kangaroos I saw on the beach the previous week, this was my first time seeing one in broad daylight, its tan coat crouched among the tall grass, feeding, and then ever so slightly hopping away. It might've been the umpteenth time Will saw one, as often and insignificant as I saw squirrels, but he acted like it was his first time too. My awe reflected in his awe as we eyed this kangaroo in the tall grass together.

SECRET BOYFRIEND

Since Wes was sick, Manang Ava had made Arroz Caldo for dinner, one of my favorite dishes.

"I love this so much," I told her.

"Your mum makes this often?" she asked as she commented how she only made it when someone was sick. It made sense considering the ingredients of chicken broth and fresh ginger were rich in antioxidants.

"I grew up eating a lot of Chicken Tinola whether anyone was sick or not. It's my favorite."

As we both knew, Chicken Tinola was a similar dish to Arroz Caldo with almost the same ingredients except Arroz Caldo's lugaw—rice porridge—was replaced by Chicken Tinola's sotanghon—mung bean thread noodles.

I realized since living in New Zealand, I hadn't made any Filipino food. I cooked often, but my college self had abandoned cooking any Filipino dishes, preferring to cook American dishes like roast chicken, pasta, or vegetable stir fry. This by far had been the longest stretch of not having any Filipino food. I could not easily go home for a weekend to enjoy my mother's home-cooked meals. I had to travel to Australia to remember what my palate had left behind.

When dishes were cleared and cleaned, and we found ourselves at the dinner table for after dinner conversation once again, I had asked Manang Ava if there were other Pinay wives like her in the area whom she might know. She told me there was one other woman in Dampier of Asian descent, but she wasn't Pinay. The woman was Chinese but Manang Ava found her husband controlling, very much unlike Mac.

I then asked her if she had ever found work in Dampier. I realize how accusatory that question must've sounded, as if a working mother still exceeded the value of a stay-at-home one.

"I briefly did the bookkeeping at the tourist shop, but it got to be too much. They wanted me to stay but I was working too many hours for little pay. It wasn't worth it. Taking care of the house and these boys is a lot of work in itself."

I remembered the older white woman with thick glasses and short gray hair who had been working behind the counter at the tourist shop earlier. Had Manang Ava had that white woman's job before it became hers?

I thought of my mother as a working mother who still cooked dinner every night. Her work ethic in the office inspired me as much as Manang Ava's work ethic in the home. The women in my family never failed to be hardworking wherever they were. With my mother, however, I could tell she was exhausted, and her husband did little to help with household chores. If there was tension between her children and her husband, she stood by in silence, as her husband yelled and called us whatever demeaning name he could think of when he was angry or disappointed in us.

My mother was incredibly proud of us, but growing up, she appeared to stand on the sidelines, as what seemed the norm for many a woman of her time and cultural upbringing. She watched her husband be the disciplinarian, the academic advisor, the academic enforcer.

Manang Ava cared about her boys' education. Concerned that her boys might not be receiving the best education she wanted for them in Dampier, she had made boarding school an option. However, the boys chose home.

Catching me off guard, Manang Ava asked me about my own prospects in a life partner. "Do you have a boyfriend?" she asked. When I replied in the affirmative, she found it odd that I did not ask to call him. "Don't you miss him? You can call him from our phone if you like."

I had just broken up with him before leaving for Australia. I wasn't ready to call him an "ex-boyfriend" just yet. I had expected that any mention of me having a boyfriend would be as nonexistent as it was back home with my parents in California. A boyfriend was non-applicable in my parents' eyes. The topic seemed equally non-applicable to any Filipino adult family member. And yet Manang Ava wanted to know. And she asked. And she wasn't mad when I told her.

As I learned through my parents' silence, there was an unspoken understanding that I wasn't to date and that my studies take precedence. My studies took precedence, but it didn't mean that I never had a boyfriend. But Manang Ava asked. Point blank. So I told her the truth.

"Are you on birth control?"

Caught off guard again, I answered, "Yes."

"That's good."

Despite my experience of knowing Filipinas of her generation—born and raised in the Philippines, indoctrinated with the rule that good Catholic girls remain virgins until marriage—Manang Ava, with her Ilocano mannerisms and accent, did not follow suit.

When I look back on being asked the birth control question, I think about if I had responded with, "It's none of your business," when I very well know that kind of answer wouldn't have flown with a cousin who was nearly my mother's age and had already established herself as a maternal authority figure over me. She had been a maternal authority figure since my infancy when I couldn't even remember her, but I innately still feared her like one. I still obeyed. The yaya-alaga relationship still carried on.

I feared what she might say about my having a boyfriend and having sex, but she was nonjudgmental and didn't condemn me for being the average twenty-year-old. Of course I had a boyfriend. Of course I had sex. And the fact of the matter didn't send her into a self-righteous, Catholic tizzy. She was a practical woman regardless of what her conservative, Catholic Motherland upbringing taught her to believe. She didn't ask me as a matter of prying. She asked me, it seemed, as a matter of concern.

It was then she mentioned the girl whom Will was possibly seeing and showed me a recent photo of the two dressed in prom attire. I assumed it was prom. The girl had blonde curls in an elegant updo and was seated in a pastel-blue ball gown. Behind her, Will stood tall and handsome, snazzy in a dark suit. With a sly smile, Manang Ava commented, "She's quite nice, isn't she?" I wondered if this was the same girl whom Will had attempted to give a hickey and failed as her skin was so pale that it barely turned any color no matter how much he sucked on her neck.

"Yes, she's lovely," I smiled.

THE LEAVING

I don't remember my goodbye with Manang Ava and her family except that I found myself back in Auckland. I would slip up and call the boyfriend. We would get back together, not in the physical sense since we were still long-distance, but I resumed what we had before.

By the time my two weeks were up in Australia, I must admit that I wasn't Manang Ava's ideal guest. I was a rude twenty-year-old. I wasn't aware that I was being rude. It wasn't my intention. I didn't offer to help wash the dishes. I didn't offer to help set the table. I didn't offer to cook dinner. And I snacked in the living room when I wasn't supposed to, and Manang Ava chastised me for it, albeit in a facetious sort of way. If I had known, I would've behaved otherwise. I was a naïve and spoiled five-year-old inside a twenty-year-old body who had yet to learn politeness and manners while staying in someone else's home.

I had yet to learn to respectfully acknowledge whose Home I was in.

Australian Aboriginal people believe that Murujuga is the starting place for "Songlines," also known as "Dreaming Tracks." These traditional stories extend back to the beginning of time, known as "the Dreaming." The Songlines are a type of verbal map or track, which describe landmarks and key events during an ancestral period, when the Earth was soft. The Songlines can be used like a road map to navigate to important sites, some extending across the continent to the eastern seaboard.

Manang Ava in Murujuga became my own starting place of learning what leaving could look like, when my mind was still impressionable, when my mind was still soft. It would take a road map of several years to fully understand and recognize my own stubbornness in trying to make an abusive relationship work simply because I did not want to be perceived a failure.

Leaving was not indicative of failure. But I didn't know any of that then. I had aimed to please as I took it as a form of accomplishment. I didn't yet see the tethered dynamic behind it.

Before dating the boyfriend, I was a poet. A prolific one too. By the time we started dating, I stopped. He didn't even inspire love poems. That should've been a sign. My writing became replaced by long weepy letters to a boy across the Pacific Ocean. When our relationship was on the verge of final collapse three years later, he admitted he hadn't read them. "They were too long," he said. Upon hearing his confession, I relived my own naïve excitement as I went to the post office in Auckland dropping off each letter, only to ultimately learn that instead of my lover tearing them open to read his girlfriend's innermost thoughts, he would open the envelope, count how many pages they were, stuff them back into the envelope, and stash them in a heap. The rest of my letters collected dust.

He finally read them when I dumped him, three years from the day when the letters had been originally written. It was a gesture to try and win me back. He didn't.

It would take years to recognize my relationships were no different from the established dynamics with my father. Friends saw the charming father and charming boyfriend. I saw the other side of the coin.

My father had huge ambitions for his daughters to be successful, which sounded feminist, but in the end, he chose the careers and lectured you on how to be an obedient wife and mother to your husband, and if you disagreed, you faced a barrage of unsolicited advice, lectures, and endless array of reminders, as if he knew your dreams better than yourself.

Despite the geographic boundaries I put between my parents, myself, and the boyfriend, the threads that remained still had their impact, making me obedient no matter where I was in the world.

Traditionally, Aboriginal people welcome visitors to their land by performing a "Welcome to Country" ceremony. The purpose is to let the land and the ancestral spirits know that someone is visiting and to ask the land and the ancestral spirits to protect the visitor. Under this protection, visitors are not only protected during their stay but also from any mischievous spirits that might follow the visitor after they have left Murujuga, "Country."

There had been no formal ceremony to welcome me to Murujuga, but I felt safe there. Even the jellyfish didn't sting. When I left, it wasn't that mischievous spirits followed me back to Auckland, but I had returned to the demons I had left behind.

Not only did my relationship worsen when I returned to California, but I would immediately apply to law school upon graduating college at my father's recommendation without carefully considering the kind of life I was resigning myself to—a kind of life that I naïvely thought was noble and glamorous but, in reality, would not always be noble and was far from glamorous.

By twenty-one, Manang Ava had already staked a claim to her life. Only decades later would I realize how tough as nails she had been to abandon a career she never wanted despite her family's expectations. She refused the courtship of certain men she didn't find attractive. She married someone she loved when it might not have met her family's particular desire or approval. And she was ready to move away from everything she had ever known to be with the person she loved. Despite the bouts of loneliness she might've experienced in Dampier with only her husband and boys as her source of companionship, she also experienced independence, a loving and equal partnership in marriage, and freedom from judgment and control that Motherland limitations and her family might have otherwise imposed upon her.

We talked about the body. We talked about the pill. We talked about periods. She talked about her pregnancies and the infertility struggles she faced as she and Mac wanted an entire football team but were blessed with two beautiful boys.

Manang Ava talked about these subjects with nonchalance—something I was still getting used to—as I learned early on in life, certain subjects were never to be discussed. But Manang Ava broached these subjects without shame.

Manang Ava, a granddaughter of an albolaryo—a well-known healer throughout our ancestral home—had dismantled a long-held silence during my stay and passed on her wealth of family knowledge to me. Ináng-bayan was our birthplace and we carried Her in our bones no matter where we were in the world, and now one great-granddaughter in Australia told another great-granddaughter from the United States things she should know for her own good.

Rather than Manang Ava's decisions inspiring me to see that my life belonged to me and no one else, her life and everything she had decided for herself seemed so far away from what I thought I was capable of achieving. I would be twenty-one in three months, yet I was still following orders across continents and oceans. An inescapable shadow of obligation followed me wherever I went. I only thought for myself in times of respite such as it was in Murujuga.

"Why didn't you just leave?"

I would hear that question over the years, not directed at me, but other women. I would even ask that question, not of myself, but other women. As if I were different.

Leaving was an uncertain road map that had several weigh stations. Like breadcrumbs, clues would be left behind, hopefully leading you to ultimately recognize your relationship for what it truly was. After each weigh station, hopefully another obstacle wouldn't impede your path and force you to backtrack. Hopefully there would be movement forward, permanently.

Only from fellow survivors would I hear the alternative, "Why didn't he just stop?"

I would continue to travel and live in various cities, hoping the shadow of obligation would eventually recede to a faint thread that would not tug me back into submission but instead serve as a road map to freedoms I finally allowed myself to have.

A daughter's forgiveness for her father would gradually arrive in the quietness at the dinner table, when she would notice her aging patriarch—his complicated vulnerability and dreams for his children's future, where he had persisted to carve out his legacy in an adopted homeland that had long been established to exclude people like us.

I haven't seen Manang Ava and her family since. I would only catch glimpses of their present-day lives through the tiny lens of social media. Manang Ava and Mac would not retire to Queensland after all, but would relocate as close as possible to their boys. The boys themselves would leave

Murujuga and spread like seeds across the Australian continent, taking root in metropolitan cities, one in Perth and the other in Adelaide. Will and Wes, the great-great-grandsons of Pedro and Petrona from Labnig, would further the Diaspora, away, away from our tiny ancestral barrio in the Philippines.

I haven't seen Dampier since. Murujuga itself would be declared a National Park in 2013, becoming the 100th National Park in Australia, and owned by the Murujuga Aboriginal Corporation, which represents the five Traditional Custodian groups of the area—Ngarluma, Yaburara, Mardudhunera, Yindjibarndi, and Wong-Goo-Tt-Oo. The national park is leased back to the Western Australian government and jointly managed by MAC and the Department of Biodiversity, Conservation and Attractions. This joint management approach under a legislative framework could be interpreted as a process of reconciliation with the Aboriginal community, coupled with federal Acknowledgment of ongoing Aboriginal connection to Country, but also non-Aboriginal reciprocal responsibility for Country. In 2018, the Western Australian government signed a statement of intention with MAC to formally pursue an application for world heritage listing for Murujuga National Park—a gesture of good faith by both parties. However, traditional owners remain skeptical. Future industrial development continues to be earmarked for the area where pollution resulting from acid rain through industry emissions, is likely to destroy the rock art over time. In 2020, the Murujuga Cultural Landscape was added to Australia's World Heritage Tentative List, but traditional owners remain wary as the government must demonstrate a commitment to protecting and monitoring the rock art through a crucial monitoring program for industrial emissions. In 2021, the Western Australian government approved to have gas pumped on the Burrup Peninsula through an interconnector pipeline, without any environmental impact assessment, without assessing the carbon pollution, and without assessing the impacts on the rock art. As of 2022, construction work on a multibillion-dollar fertilizer plant threatens further desecration of Murujuga's ancient petroglyphs under the government's purview.

Reconciliation, alongside gaslighting, manipulation, and oppression, can be an ongoing tightrope, whether it be between governments and peoples, between fathers and daughters, between intimate partners, or just with oneself.

When my sixteen-month-old self had left my Motherland, I wouldn't say I left. For the betterment of our lives and our futures, my parents carried me to whatever land I was brought to. There were no explanations. No apologies.

But in Murujuga is the first time I left. I. Left.

Absent phone calls, letters, and emails, the two weeks I had spent in Murujuga was the first time I left. I. Left.

Lilong had been right all along that I should meet Manang Ava in Dampier.

Murujuga had marked the beginning of leaving. And when it comes to leaving, we have to start somewhere.

PREVIOUS PUBLICATIONS

in order of the Table of Contents, previous versions have appeared in the following

"First Home," *Unbound: An Anthology on Composing Home*, Minnesota State University Moorhead: New Rivers Press, 2022

"One Hundred and Eighty Eggs," *Hairstreak Butterfly Review*, 2021

"Bad Pro-Choicer," *Anomaly*, 2019

"When The Body Speaks," *MUTHA Magazine*, 2022

"Giving Birth in a Time of War," *Cherry Tree*, 2020

"Stone," finalist for the Lamar York Prize for Nonfiction sponsored by *The Chattahoochee Review*, 2019

RECOMMENDED READING

ONE HUNDRED AND EIGHTY EGGS

"Past As Present: America's Sordid History of Medical Reproductive Abuse and Experimentation." *National Partnership for Women and Families*, 1 Oct. 2020. https://www.nationalpartnership.org/our-work/resources/health-care/past-as-present-americas-sordid-history-of-medical-reproductive-abuse-and-experimentation.pdf

LAST THREE DAYS IN TWENTYNINE PALMS

Cultural Systems Research, Inc. "The Native Americans of Joshua Tree National Park: An Ethnographic Overview and Assessment Study." *The National Park Service*, 22 Aug. 2002, www.nps.gov/parkhistory/online_books/jotr/history3.htm#:~:text=The%20peoples%20who%20occupied%20and,the%20Mojave%2C%20and%20the%20Chemehuevi

"History of TwentyNine Palms Band of Mission Indians." *TwentyNine Palms Band of Mission Indians: The Official Tribal Government Website*, 2020, www.29palmstribe.org/copy-of-our-mission-statement-1

"Our City's Native American Past." *City of Carson, California Official Website*, 2021, ci.carson.ca.us/aboutcarson/nativeamerican.aspx

Trafzer, Clifford E. *A Chemehuevi Song: Resiliency of the Southern Paiute Tribe*. Seattle: University of Washington Press, 2015

THE BEGINNING OF LEAVING

"About Our Land." *Murujuga Aboriginal Corporation (MAC)*, www.murujuga.org.au/our-land/our-land/

Collins, Ben. "How Explorer and Pirate William Dampier's Comments on Aboriginal People in 1697 Set the Tone for Future Sentiment." *Australian Broadcasting Corporation News*, 3 Nov. 2018. https://www.abc.net.au/news/2018-11-04/william-dampiers-terra-nullius-set-the-tone-for-australia/10420338

Coughlan, Matt. "Pauline Hanson Again Slammed for Racism." *The Canberra Times*, 12 Feb. 2020. https://www.canberratimes.com.au/story/6628133/pauline-hanson-again-slammed-for-racism/

Evershed, Nick. "Frontier Massacres: Role of Australia's Colonial Government Forces Revealed – Datablog." *The Guardian*, 4 Mar. 2019. https://www.theguardian.com/australia-news/ng-interactive/2019/mar/05/frontier-massacres-role-of-australias-colonial-government-forces-revealed-datablog

Hastie, Hamish. "Woodside Gets State Backing to Pump Gas from Pluto to Karratha Gas Plant." *The Sydney Morning Herald*, 29 Jan. 2021. https://www.smh.com.au/business/companies/woodside-gets-state-backing-to-pump-gas-from-pluto-to-karratha-gas-plant-20210129-p56xt8.html

Milne, Peter. "Controversial $6.5b Burrup Fertiliser Plant to Get Green Light by the End of the Year." *WA Today*, 1 Oct. 2022. https://www.watoday.com.au/national/western-australia/controversial-6-5b-burrup-fertiliser-plant-to-get-green-light-by-the-end-of-the-year-20220930-p5bm9l.html

"Murujuga National Park." *Explore Parks WA, Government of Western Australia*, exploreparks.dbca.wa.gov.au/park/murujuga-national-park

"National Heritage Places - Dampier Archipelago (Including Burrup Peninsula)." *Australian Government: Department of Climate Change, Energy, the Environment and Water*, 3 Oct. 2021, www.dcceew.gov.au/parks-heritage/heritage/places/national/dampier-archipelago

"Page Law (1875)." *The University of Texas at Austin, Department of History, College of Liberal Arts, A Project of the Immigration and Ethnic History Society*, 2019, https://immigrationhistory.org/item/page-act/

Page Act of 1875 (Immigration Act), Forty-Third Congress. Sess. II. Ch. 141. 1875

"Welcome to Country? | Jade Kennedy | TEDxUWollongong." *YouTube,* uploaded by TEDx Talks, 12 Nov. 2018, www.youtube.com/watch?v=BdYmSByzrL8

Weber, David. "Woodside Faces Challenge Over Burrup Hub LNG Plans Amid Pollution and Rock Art Fears." *Australian Broadcasting Corporation News*, 20 Dec. 2020. https://www.abc.net.au/news/2020-12-21/woodside-faces-burrup-gas-fight-amid-rock-art-pollution-fears/13003532

Young, Emma. "WA Cuts Loose Burrup Rock Art Monitors for Breaching $7 Million Contract, Considers Limiting Industry." *The Sydney Morning Herald*, 10 Jun. 2021. https://www.smh.com.au/business/companies/wa-cuts-loose-rock-art-monitors-for-breaching-7-million-contract-20210609-p57zjj.html

Zaunmayr, Tom. "Flying Foam Massacre Milestone Remembered." *Pilbara News*, 16 Apr. 2018. https://www.pilbaranews.com.au/news/pilbara-news/flying-foam-massacre-milestone-remembered-ng-b88800011z

ACKNOWLEDGMENTS

Thank you to my diligent, patient, and inimitable editor, Emily Perkovich, at Querencia Press, for seeing value in these stories so they may be shared in the Diaspora. And of course, infinite gratitude for the arduous task of polishing this manuscript with your meticulousness and utmost care so that it shines.

To the literary journals and editors who first made homes for these pieces, with special thanks to editors Nayt Rundquist, Cheryl Klein, Genevieve Pfeiffer, Sarah Clark, and Lindsay Lusby, for being the first pair of diligent eyes to provide feedback for my work.

To all the readers who sent the most encouraging messages and believed in my storytelling.

To those unnamed but were catalysts for writing these stories down, especially those who reminded me that our ancestors remain with us as we birth our stories.

To Gladys Nadal Somera, it's taken two and a half decades to touch base but our ancestors would be so pleased to know that we found each other again. Thank you for reaching out, my beautiful kasinsin.

To Andy Guerrero, for helping me unpack heaviness from long ago and most importantly, helping me weed out colonialist structures in our writing when they insidiously seep through. And of course, immortalized love for not one, but TWO late night Mary-Shelley-extravaganzas.

To Morgan Hoffman, am certain our La Union Great-Lolas—Isabel and Clara—from Ubbog and Agoo are finally exhaling as their descendant great-granddaughters meeting in the Diaspora finally arrived. Little Springs and Whistling Pines kasinsins unite.

To Pauline Shand who always knew I was writing way before we even met.

To Caren Ang-oay who keeps me connected to the archipelago of my birth.

To Natanya Pulley who sent the most reaffirming message that reinforced my belief in the intersections of our lands, our ancestors, and our peoples, no matter how many oceans apart.

To Juanita E. Mantz whose own stories remind me to birth my own with compassion and care.

To Veronica Montes and Jean Vengua, for your thoughtful and uplifting words. If our Diaspora had words to describe you, you would be the high priestesses of our times.

To Eliza Gano, my darling love, always for your wisdom, presence, and support.

To Shane, for the check-ins across hemispheres. Pedro and Petrona would be happy to know that the Diaspora doesn't keep their descendants apart.

Unending gratitude to my bloodline in Australia—Manang Wilma, Mal, Chris, and Shane—for your hospitality in Dampier that this twenty-year-old kid will never forget.

To Auntie Maggie, for those early stories about the great Ilocos Sur migration. You are a treasure trove of our history.

To Lolo Doming, Lola Fely, Lilong Tito, and Lilang Atang, who still speak to me from the Great Unknown.

To Josh, for all that is left behind, and remains, this was a hard book to write. Thank you for taking care of us while I locked myself away working on this collection.

To Daddy, for teaching me the intersections between our ancestral soil and the need for ongoing environmental care as practiced by our ancestors for thousands of years, and for keeping me connected to our Somera, Torres, and Valmidiano bloodlines at Home and in the Diaspora.

Last, to Ma, for being my Ilocano and Tagalog interpreter; for being my Queen of her own brilliant Sarsarita; for being the conjurer of our beloved Carig and Orejudos ancestors; and for being the conjurer of her Ma, and most importantly, her Pa, whom she keeps alive through questions and stories and dreams.